THE DIVERSITY DILEMMA

DR. THELÁ R. THATCH

Copyright © 2023 Thelá R. Thatch, Ph.D.

All Rights Reserved. This book contains material protected under International and Federal Copyright Laws and Treaties. Any unauthorized reprint or use of this material is prohibited. No part of this book may be reproduced or transmitted in any form or by any means, electronic or mechanical, including photocopying, recording, or by any information storage and retrieval system without express written permission from the author/publisher.

ISBNs:
Hardcover: 979-8-218-33434-5
Paperback: 979-8-89079-080-4
Ebook: 979-8-89079-081-1

Thatched Roof Publishing

DEDICATION

This book is dedicated to everyone who has struggled with communicating their frustration with diversity, equity, inclusion, and belonging and just could not put their finger on what was wrong. Thank you to my family – my partner Norman, my children Simone, Chris, and Anthony, my grandson Jayden, and our Siberian Huskies, Cairo, and Brooklyn, for your support. Thank you to my parents, Richard and Theola Hosten; your struggles were not in vain.

A special shout-out to Avis Ann Jenkins for her friendship and her commitment to see this book to fruition.

To April Colbert-Ramirez, you have been the wind beneath my wings.

To Dr. Anna Nikki Douglas, words cannot express my gratitude for your brilliance and editorial genius. Thank you.

I wrote this book for Black, Brown, and Tan people and anyone who has been marginalized.

I dedicate this book to every publisher and everyone who could not understand the relevance of this book.

Thank you for making me stronger and more determined to write and publish it.

The Diversity Dilemma: A Survivor's Guide for Diversity and Inclusion Good Doers
by
Dr. Thelá R. Thatch, PHR, SHRM-CP

Mandatory diversity training? Hastily developed initiatives. Has the recent focus on diversity and inclusion done more harm than good?

The Diversity Dilemma is a no-holds-barred account of the impact of work on diversity on society, culture, community, and humanity. Dr. Thela Thatch, a Human Resource expert with over 25 years of working with Fortune 500 companies, explores the damage caused to people and organizational culture, all in the name of diversity. Thatch writes from the center of the diversity, equity, and inclusion (DEI) dilemma—where efforts to correct glaring issues simultaneously clash with the painful consequences of exposing them. This deep dive investigates whether the spotlight on DEI has truly moved the needle forward or further polarized and exacerbated pre-existing diversity and inclusion issues.

The Diversity Dilemma is a call to action for leaders, HR professionals, and employees committed to diversity, equity, and inclusion. It serves as both a challenge and encouragement for those dedicated to driving lasting change in these areas. This book is for employee resource group leaders, human resource professionals, leaders, and followers who have given their all for the sake of equity and inclusion. Dr. Thatch provides an honest look into why the diversity movement and actions prompted by this understating have seen little modulation in the past two decades. After being tapped on the shoulder to lead DEI initiatives, Dr. Thatch looked at the damage done to people and organizational culture along the way—all done in the name of diversity.

Dr. Thatch prompts readers to reflect on whether the ongoing emphasis on diversity has led to a counterproductive state of polarization, hindering rather than aiding inclusion efforts. The dilemma arises as readers grapple with addressing issues related to respect and differences, while also confronting the repercussions of a lack of diversity and minimal understanding of inclusion.

FOREWORDS

As Executive Director of the Los Angeles African American Women's Public Policy Institute (LAAAWPPI) for the past 21 years, I administer this program which is a leadership development/public policy instruction program focusing on African American women looking to be more involved in civic engagement and public policy. Our graduates are tackling the issues of inclusion, investigating opportunities to enhance their communities, and trying to develop employment opportunities that showcase their talents. Our 384 graduates are starting businesses, becoming involved in politics, starting community-based organizations, and working their way up the corporate ladder through the departments of public policy and community development. In getting started on the road to success, they must face obstacles of equity when applying for jobs, in seeking funding for a business, getting support for non-profit projects, and applying for promotions in their current employment. There is frustration, and there are successes. Dr. Thelá Thatch's book will most certainly enhance the opportunities for success!

Dr. Thelá Thatch is "spot on" when describing the good, the bad, and the ugly, but most importantly, the significance of Diversity, Equity, and Inclusion (DEI) and what such a program can positively accomplish in business, government, and community enhancement. Dr. Thatch is tackling the DEI issue from a corporate framework; however, governments, non-profits, and foundations are jumping onto the DEI bandwagon without fully recognizing the vast potential that DEI can offer communities. Many entities just say, "We have to get this DEI term in the books immediately and prove our support for social justice and equity." But what does that mean?

As my friend Thelá points out, a well-equipped DEI program does not just appoint a DEI manager but also allocates significant funds and resources to develop a staff and program that creates an effective, comprehensive inclusion program. She effectively outlines the necessary steps vital to implementing and sustaining a DEI program that values the talent, ingenuity, and creativeness of our society as a whole.

Dr. Thatch's book is born out of frustration at not REALLY UNDERSTANDING what a comprehensive DEI initiative is composed of. By developing this book, *The Diversity Dilemma: A Survivor's Guide for Diversity Good Doers*, she brings to the forefront the important role that diversity plays in hiring practices in an environment of a truly diverse society. A good DEI program can be effective in developing practices that help maintain a thriving, healthy, and successful work and community environment.

I look forward to providing LAAAWPPI classes with Dr. Thelá Thatch's solid and informative book!

~Joy P. Atkinson
Commissioner, City of Los Angeles &
Executive Director of the Los Angeles African American
Women's Public Policy Institute (LAAAWPPI)

***

Dr. Thelá Thatch was one of the first DEIB thought leaders I met when I relocated to Los Angeles from New York. I intentionally wanted to build my network in my new hometown with Black women who were in my space and doing this work within the confines of the walls of corporate America. She quickly became my "shero" because she did not shy away from speaking truth to power and removing herself from high-profile positions that no longer served her. Therefore, I am not the least bit surprised that she decided to share her experiences in such a candid way in her new book, *Diversity Dilemma*.

DEIB work has been a constant challenge for corporate America to grapple with ever since Black Xerox employees started the first Black Employee Resource Group in 1970. Unfortunately, not much has changed over 50 years later. Hiring Black and Brown people to man the front lines of this work has been a well-played performative act that has resulted in high mental and emotional tax for these professionals, with many of them leaving their positions after relatively short terms. Trying to influence change from the inside is not for the weak or weary, but prioritizing your well-being, safety, and peace should not be left at the threshold of those revolving doors.

Dr. Thelá has taken the baton for all of us DEIB thought leaders. Through her candid perspective shared in this book, she challenges corporate leaders to look in the mirror and honestly assess their commitment in words compared to their commitment in action. She has been on the front lines of many well-known Fortune 500 organizations and has personally witnessed what works and what does not work in DEIB for both the employees and the DEIB leaders of those organizations.

Her voice is needed now more than ever as we witness the pendulum swing so far away from the real intent and purpose of DEIB, primarily due to fear of change and equity for all employees. I applaud Dr. Thelá for putting it all on the line and taking us through her DEIB journey while also dropping much-needed gems for organizational leaders to keep in mind as they look at their internal initiatives around this important work.

Dr. Thelá - the current and future workforce thanks you for your ongoing commitment to this work and for your grit, determination, and resiliency while remaining humble and a beacon of light for us all!

~ Dr. Tana M. Sessions, CEO/ Founder, TMS Business Solutions, Inc; DEI Strategist, International Speaker, Corporate Trainer; author of *Working While Black: A Woman's Guide to Stop Being the Best Kept Secret*

***

Dr. Thelá Thatch, an exemplary example of a leader who places care and empathy at the forefront of all she does, is perfect to author this book. Sharing her over 25 years of experience to engage a diverse audience that will reach the masses and spread authenticity and a solid teaching of leadership and equity is invaluable. As a leader of today, Dr. Thatch provides a fresh perspective that includes the courageous exploration of experiences that many others would not dare to share in public. She changes the narrative around the unspoken rules and inequities that exist in our workplaces and social interactions. She sheds light on her traumatic experiences, much like those of people from marginalized groups that usually go unseen and unheard.

I have had the pleasure of working with Dr. Thatch as a practitioner on a variety of projects focused on creating a structured approach to diversity, equity, and inclusion. Most often, the projects were just that, projects and not real efforts for change, transparency, and accountability. After exhausting all resources, having several conversations with key leaders, and developing clear plans of action, our efforts were rarely realized. We have confronted the diversity dilemma together, and there is nothing more disheartening than realizing the thing you felt was within reach is farther than you have imagined. With those sad realities, Dr. Thatch continues to pursue justice and pushes to create environments where all can thrive.

Each place she spreads her magic is forever changed, and this book is no different.

Without a fight, there is no glory. Dr. Thatch motivates DEI and HR practitioners to persist in advocating for concrete results that empower those without a voice. As practitioners of this work, we are often faced with the dilemma of being authentic to the work we do or standing in allegiance with organizations that have half-heartedly taken on these initiatives as a performative measure to increase market share or position themselves as progressive. This book offers a roadmap to encourage practitioners to take a stance when the dilemma of diversity has become too much to bear. This book offers insights on how to strategically use influence to get results that change lives and humanity.

Seeking change around diversity, equity, and inclusion within America's workplaces can be a daunting task unlike any other organizational initiative. It requires the organization to take a long and honest look at the role they have played and continue to play in the injustice of those that present as different. The stereotypes, biases, and hate that surround these groups are inherently engrained in our society. Understanding the impact of these things within an organization usually requires an analysis and examination of racism and discrimination as well as a revelation of how it shows up in the organizational culture. This realization is something that most organizations struggle with, and it is often the responsibility of the DEI leader to address.

The choice of how to address these issues can cause an internal battle among many practitioners, as there is a fear of retaliation and alienation. However, there is also an overwhelming feeling to do what is right for people. This is an example of the diversity dilemma, and unfortunately, fear habitually wins. Dr. Thatch offers her experiences as a Black woman in corporate America and provides tools to help us remain authentic and courageous in this fight we call diversity, equity, and inclusion work.

This book is a celebration of the freedom of overcoming the diversity dilemma, the continued fight for justice, and the invaluable skill of never giving up. This book is just in time as we continue to experience a tremendous shift in how and why we work. It is a highly valuable resource in an area that needs more guidance. Thank you, Dr. Thatch!

~ Dr. Deanna Kimbrel,
Kimbrel Management Consulting

CONTENTS

INTRODUCTION:
Defining Our Diversity Dilemma — xv

Part 1: DEFINING — 1

I. THE POWER OF A WORD — 17
II. TRAUMA AND DRAMA — 64
III. FACT OR FICTION — 79

Part 2: DISRUPTING — 83

IV. THE PRICE TO PAY — 87
V. AFFIRMING ACTION — 94
VI. THE LIES & THE TRUTH ABOUT IMPOSTER SYNDROME — 101

Part 3: DECIDING — 109

VII. DIE IN HR DEI — 111
VIII. POLICY FORCES CHANGE — 137
IX. REAL EQUITY — 144
X. RECRUITING FOR INCLUSION — 148
XI. THE ROAD TO INCLUSION — 157

Appendix — 185
Vocabulary — 191
About the Author — 195

INTRODUCTION
DEFINING OUR DIVERSITY DILEMMA

Debacle — a sudden and ignominious failure; a fiasco. Initially, I wanted this book to be titled The Diversity Debacle. Then, I thought, "…it hasn't been a complete failure." However, we are facing a dilemma. By the very definition of the word, a dilemma is a situation in which a person or group faces two or more conflicting options or choices, each of which may have both positive and negative consequences. It typically involves a problematic decision-making process because choosing one option often means sacrificing the benefits of the other.

Dilemmas can arise in various contexts, including personal, ethical, moral, or professional. They often present individuals with a sense of being torn between two equally compelling or undesirable alternatives, making it challenging to determine the most appropriate course of action. Resolving a dilemma often requires careful consideration of each choice's potential outcomes and implications and the values, principles, and priorities that impact those choices. The real dilemma is that the choices that are being made around diversity affect the population that needs it the most.

The term *diversity dilemma* is not a specific concept and can be used in various contexts. However, it generally refers to the challenges and tensions that arise when attempting to promote diversity, equity, and inclusion within organizations or societies. These dilemmas often involve balancing the need for representation and inclusion of under-represented groups with potential conflicts, such as differing perspectives, power dynamics, or resistance to change. *The Diversity Dilemma* highlights the complexities and trade-offs in fostering diversity while navigating these challenges.

The term diversity dilemma lacks a specific originator but has gained widespread usage in conversations and literature centered around diversity and inclusion. It characterizes the intricate challenges linked with effectively managing diversity across different situations. This predicament emerges during discussions about diversity and equity, as these concepts frequently involve tough choices or compromises. Pursuing diversity entails fostering representation and inclusivity among individuals from various backgrounds and perspectives. Conversely, equity emphasizes furnishing equitable opportunities and outcomes for all, particularly those historically disadvantaged.

THE RACE DILEMMA

The present situation underscores the long-deferred "40 acres and a mule" promise. Unfortunately, there is a noticeable apprehension that this commitment might never come to fruition. Imagine what would happen if reparations were bestowed; the resulting economic prosperity would be unparalleled. Acquiring financial strategies tailored to our needs is vital to constructing self-sufficient communities.

In reality, research conducted by McKinsey in their report titled *The Emerging Black Consumer* exposed the lower income and wealth experienced by Black households. Despite making up 13.4% of the United States population, Black households accounted for slightly less than 10% of the nation's total expenditure on goods and services in 2019. With reduced earnings, Black workers grapple with diminished financial means each month, particularly when considering debt. The absence of diverse perspectives and experiences in decision-making has obstructed the development of inclusive policies, exacerbating income inequality for Black individuals, and perpetuating economic disparities. Nevertheless, certain companies misinterpreted this data as evidence that catering to Black consumers was not lucrative. These companies are making a significant misjudgment.

Many years of underserving the Black community have created significant opportunities for companies willing to look beneath the surface. There are two effective strategies for companies to pursue: expanding local access to goods and services and creating offerings better tailored to Black households' needs and preferences. Companies filling these needs could tap into $300 billion of value annually. That is a significant reason for innovative companies in the United States and globally to not overlook the importance of diversity.

According to Nielson, of the nearly 50 million Black people in the United States, Black consumers spend more than $1 trillion a year. According to a recent McKinsey report, the combined spending by all Black households has increased 5% annually over the past two decades. It has outpaced the growth rate of combined spending by White households by 2%. White Americans hold 84% of total United States wealth but make up only 60% of the population—while

Black Americans hold 4% of the wealth and make up 13% of the population. Racial wealth inequality has been pervasive in the United States since the earliest days of colonization.

Despite constitutional guarantees of equality and numerous anti-discrimination laws, racial wealth gaps persist and are widening. Black Americans are incarcerated in state prisons at nearly five times the rate of White Americans. Nationally, 1 in 81 Black adults in the United States are serving time in state prison. Wisconsin leads the nation in Black imprisonment rates; 1 in 36 Black Wisconsinites are in prison.

For the first time in history, we see widespread movement around racism following the murder of George Floyd. There have been countless protests against racist practices, an uptake in DEI programs throughout most industries, and a barrage of race-fueled opinions emitted across social media platforms in the past few years. We have experienced the first Black President and the first Black female Vice President. However, we have not arrived. We have shifted from a history of Jim Crow racism to overt color-blind racism. It is not about WHETHER race matters, but HOW race matters. We now look at police, institutions, and organizations through a historical lens—a very jaded historical lens.

Black people have been criminalized for over 400 years. Brown bodies have been made to feel inferior and subjected to brutal force. Brutal force against Brown bodies has been normalized. In the mid-1600s, White men were often deputized as police officers. This allowed White men to be imbued with the power to hunt runaway slaves; another form of racism by those in power.

The early 20th century saw the establishment of the Ku Klux Klan and the Great Migration. The Great Migration was a period in which Blacks in the South moved to the North in droves. This migration marked a period of growth for Black Americans. In turn, the Ku Klux Klan terrorized Black people by burning crosses and even lynching those who "broke the law."

By understanding the history of racism, then you can further understand the current dilemma. The intergenerational transmission of oppression complicates the implementation of DEI initiatives. If you are reading this and thinking, "Here we go, more race talks; I'm tired of it," you need to keep reading because you are a part of the problem.

TOXIC WORK CULTURE

When I started my journey in diversity work as a Human Resources professional, I was warned that I would get fired. Since then, not only have I been fired, but I have also been pushed out, marginalized, harassed, and attacked for striving for diversity. I felt the invisible target on my back and was warned early on to get used to it. So, in this book, we will learn and revisit language and thoughts that I could have used then and words that I use now to even the playing field for those on the equity battlefield. Terms such as *credible messengers*, *collateral consequences*, and other vocabulary aid in deconstructing systems created against us. Phrases related to employee attrition such as *quiet quitting*, *grind culture*, and *she-cession* are increasing.

According to the Bureau of Labor Statistics, three million women have left the workforce since February 2020. This phenomenon has been called *she-cession*. She-cession refers to the economic downturn disproportionately impacting women, particularly in terms of job losses and setbacks in employment. The term highlights the gendered impact of economic challenges, such as those experienced during recessions or crises. This is where women may face higher rates of unemployment or reduced workforce participation compared to men. The she-cession underscores the need to address and understand the specific challenges faced by women in the workforce during times of economic uncertainty.

The Great Resignation of 2021, also known as the Big Quit, the Great Reshuffle, and the Great Reflection, is another phenomenon where employees voluntarily resigned from their jobs *en masse*. Wage stagnation, a rising cost of living, limited opportunities for career advancement, hostile work environments, and strict remote work policies are the most cited reasons for resignation.

Consider Billie, one of the 4.3 million individuals who left their jobs by August 2021, as reported by the Department of Labor. Despite working at her dream job creating graphics for a marketing firm, Billie faced challenges such as long hours, unreasonable demands, and questionable practices that conflicted with her personal values. Billie's experience reflects a shifting social contract between employees and employers. As we move beyond the pandemic, there is an observable transition in power dynamics from employer-centric to employee-centric.

Now, let us look at the trend of *quiet quitting*, where employees are not leaving a job outright but doing precisely what the position requires, the minimum and no more. According to a recent Gallup poll, up to 50% of American workers have quietly quit their jobs. We are seeing a cultural shift in how United States employees approach work. Employees are moving away from the hustle-and-grind mentality and focusing more on their work-life integration, job satisfaction, and physical and mental health.

Diversity in the workplace impacts the mental health of its employees. According to the Centers for Disease Control (CDC), about 1 in 5 American adults experience a mental illness yearly. That means 20% of our workforce is affected by mental illness. Compounding this statistic, the CDC also reports that people in some racial and ethnic minority groups face obstacles to maintaining positive mental health.

Grind culture and *invisible work* (work that goes unnoticed and unacknowledged) adversely affect women and minorities. These practices are rooted in capitalism and White supremacy. Capitalism has impacted and impounded the dilemma around diversity. Capitalism has had a complex and varied impact on minorities in America. While capitalism has provided opportunities for economic advancement and entrepreneurship, it has also perpetuated systemic inequalities and marginalized certain groups. In terms of economic disparities, historically minorities (particularly Black and Latinos) have faced significant economic disadvantages due to a history of discrimination, including limited access to resources, education, and capital. This has resulted in persistent wealth gaps, income inequalities, and limited economic mobility.

I want to address the following areas and trends in DEI: fatigue and disinterest. This is where DEI and staff wonder when real action will be taken. Also, there is a sentiment that some need to talk to a different audience instead of "preaching to the choir."

Overall, there is a trend that people want to avoid the topic of DEI progress, especially since there has been no real change. Then, there is the dilemma of certain groups feeling targeted rather than leaning in. The challenge lies in balancing the pursuit of diversity with the goal of equity. Sometimes, efforts to increase diversity can unintentionally overlook or undermine equity by simply focusing on numbers or superficial representation.

On the other hand, prioritizing equity may involve implementing policies that can limit specific opportunities to address past disparities, which some perceive as unfair. Additionally, perspectives on what constitutes diversity and equity can vary among individuals and groups, leading to further complexity in navigating these discussions. Cultural, social, and political factors influence how people perceive and approach these issues, adding to the dilemma. The difficulty when discussing diversity and equity arises from finding the right balance between promoting representation and addressing historical disadvantages while considering differing viewpoints and potential trade-offs.

Organizations can seize the opportunity to be well-prepared in addressing applicants' inquiries regarding the company's diversity. The workplace culture and environment of an organization are crucial considerations for incoming employees. Savvy applicants may seek information on these aspects before progressing in the interview process or accepting a job offer, emphasizing the importance of organizations being ready to provide meaningful insights.

Even if you decide not to address diversity during the interview, an applicant may have a different plan. For example, I recently had a conversation with a Black woman (we shall call her Tiana) who shared that even though the risk of not being hired might be involved, she would still ask about the organization's diversity. Tiana shared:

> "If there were no People of Color in management, I would ask why. I would ask about the retention rate of managers of color... Someone in the interview process may not know these answers, and asking the questions may scare them off. But that would be a good indication of whether or not I would want to be at that company anyway. I never want to experience anything like what I did with five years in retail again. So, it is imperative in an interview process that I be open about what my expectations are.

When I came here, I said I must have the opportunity for advancement."

As leaders, you must realize that questions about diversity in the workplace may not have one appropriate response because the questions will come from various perspectives. Training your interview team on how to respond will prepare them to respond appropriately and professionally.

In my earlier years, I aspired to emulate fictional female figures like Mary Tyler Moore and Murphy Brown (both from TV shows of the same names), envisioning myself as a powerful businesswoman confidently striding down the hall to my corner office. Despite years of aspiring and working towards my goals, I observed my White counterparts receiving promotions and accolades while I struggled. Now, I have found the courage to speak up and share my story.

I write this book for Black women like me who helped others achieve merit and promotion but could not find it for themselves. This book is for Indigenous people who have watched everyone take over their land, which is now called the United States of America.

I write this book for my dark chocolate 'sistahs' that, no matter how hard they have tried, will never pass European standards, and should not have to. To my fellow lighter-skinned sisters, I express love, acknowledging the privilege our skin tone entails. I am also aware of how colorism affects our self-esteem, leading us to judge ourselves more critically than our non-Black counterparts.

This book is for all People of Color – the spectrum of melanin, representative of many cultures and continents converging. Those who have been oppressed and marginalized.

This book is for the most feared, hated, and misunderstood in all the world: my Black men. I have Black men in my life. I know and love Black men. As a 25-year corporate

HR professional, I can attest that many organizations do not. Kudos to my Black men that have climbed the rank. We know it did not happen without leaving a part of your soul behind.

It has been said that if you want to advance racial equity, prioritize the needs of Black women. It has been said and proven that if you want to advance racial equity, prioritizing the needs of Black women is not just a necessary step but a transformative approach that holds the potential to create meaningful and lasting change. Black women have historically borne the brunt of intersecting inequalities rooted in race and gender, enduring systemic discrimination that often goes unnoticed or unaddressed. By centering our experiences, challenges, and aspirations, society can understand the multifaceted nature of inequality and work towards dismantling the structures that perpetuate it.

Black women have consistently been at the forefront of social justice movements, advocating for the rights of both their racial and gender communities. We face unique challenges that encompass both racial bias and gender-based discrimination, often resulting in a compounded impact that affects various aspects of our lives, from healthcare and education to employment and representation. Prioritizing our needs in policymaking, resource allocation, and advocacy efforts is a recognition of our invaluable contributions and a commitment to rectifying historical injustices.

Moreover, focusing on the needs of Black women is a strategic choice with broad-reaching implications. The liberation and empowerment of Black women can trigger a ripple effect that uplifts entire communities. As primary caregivers, community leaders, and change agents, our progress can catalyze positive changes in families, neighborhoods, and beyond. By addressing the specific challenges faced by Black women, such as maternal mortality rates, wage disparities, and limited access to quality education, society can pave the way for a more just and equitable future for everyone.

In essence, advancing racial equity is intricately tied to recognizing Black women's unique struggles and strengths. By prioritizing our needs, society acknowledges the interconnectedness of various forms of discrimination and commits to dismantling the structures that perpetuate inequality. This approach not only honors the contributions of Black women to social progress but also leverages our empowerment as a catalyst for broader systemic change. As we build a fairer world, it becomes clear that centering the needs of Black women is not just a step but a transformative leap toward achieving true equity and justice for all.

I want to tell this story from the perspective of a Black woman whose life is the point of focus of most equity initiatives. It is lives like mine that we aim to correct. I want to tell my story with my voice in hopes that those doing this work hear their voice and see themselves. The story of a young girl from East Orange, New Jersey, born in East Orange General Hospital to two young parents who almost had a fighting chance. To parents who did not know the extent to which the system was rigged against them. My mom did not understand feminism, but she attempted to express her freedom as a woman in how she dressed and moved. My mom did not have the tools as she struggled to claim her rights in a society that was not ready to release her.

The impact this had on my parents was detrimental. My dad barely escaped the horrors of the Vietnam War by avoiding the draft, only to see his brother succumb to the atrocities of the same war. Instead, my dad enrolled as a police officer and was taught how to fight a war against his people on the streets of East Orange. Good people my dad would eventually exploit as he succumbed to alcohol and drug addiction. Heroin was his drug of choice and demise.

Consequently, these factors affected the way I showed up and how I was seen in the workplace and the world.

I want to share how I worked my tail off, sacrificed, and rose to the top - only to be sent spiraling down. I learned that my story is like many Black women who believe that hard work is all we need. I want this book to be a place of refuge and a complementary companion to regular therapy sessions. A part of the healing process for those damaged and traumatized by failed diversity initiatives. This book is a statement and confirmation that you are not crazy. Real things have happened to you. Most of all, I want this book to remind you and confirm that you are enough and have always been. Two master's degrees and a Ph.D. later, you might say, "That is easy for you to say, Dr. Thatch. I am doing what I need to survive." If you are someone who finds themselves merely surviving, I want you to discover the solace and resources I lacked when embarking on my journey to advocate for and implement equity in my workplaces. At times, I believed the initiatives were unsuccessful due to my perceived incompetence. Despite my passion for equity, I felt I lacked strategic influence. I want you to emerge not just surviving but fully recognizing your inherent worth and knowing that you are more than enough.

What I share in this book may challenge you, and you may decide that you do not have the professional courage to do anything, nor the energy to stand, or even be the best version of yourself. That, too, is more than enough. Again, I have been where many of you have been.

I hope and pray that through this book, you feel a little stronger, a little more equipped, a little saner: that you will feel the call of your ancestors telling you that you are enough, that your work is not in vain. I hope that what feels like your failures to push the needle around justice, equity, diversity, and inclusion (JEDI), DEI, civil rights, or whatever you are calling equity initiatives right now, are making the way and movement toward incremental change.

So, please stay with me and join me on this journey behind the veil. What really happens at these "amazing" companies that we see bragging about their DEI initiatives? There are so many things happening behind the scenes. In fact, as much as some things have changed – so much remains the same. Ecclesiastes 1:9 states, "What has been, will be again. What has been done will be done again; there is nothing new under the sun."

PART I
DEFINING

> "To be a Negro in this country and to be relatively conscious is to be in a rage almost all the time."
> —James Baldwin

I am writing this book as a Black woman who is entirely and infinitely angry. I repeat, I am timelessly mad. I often say I am not the stereotypical angry Black woman; I am just angry. There IS a difference. Maybe it would help to compare my anger to that of a White woman who is angry about the injustice in the world and how there is war in Ukraine and all over the world at any given time. Or how she sometimes feels that she and her children are perpetually unsafe. This White woman is sad and angry when she thinks about these injustices. This is the same anger I feel, but it lives in Black skin. My Black anger seems to frighten people. Whereas a White woman's anger typically does not. I intentionally express my anger repeatedly because it mirrors a combination of frustration and sadness. My anger is like that of my non-Black counterparts.

The names will not be held to protect the innocent because there are no innocents. However, names will be withheld to protect my family and financial stability. Because lawsuits are expensive and not fun. Rest assured, you will read the truth about my experience and things I have seen with my eyes in over 35 years in corporate organizations. And, if you peek at my LinkedIn page, you can feel free to guess which organizations I may or may not be addressing. No one can stop you from making assumptions and good guesses. Additionally, if these experiences resonate with you or the shared experiences of another Black or Brown friend, consider what your restorative action(s) will be.

In my working experiences, I have been passed over, called an Aunt Thomasina (female version of an Uncle Tom), an Oreo (Black on the outside and White in the middle), someone who is "too big for my britches," not strategic enough, too aggressive, not vocal enough, too vocal, wishy-washy, a flip-flopper, a token, a brown noser and more. These names were based on biases and assumptions about how I should be showing up as a Black woman. Now, it is time to heal. Time to put language to experience and experience to action.

A recent report from Culture Amp's 2022 Workplace DEI Report shows that the companies that value DEI are not investing at the proper levels to drive change. The research shows that while many companies believe that DEI is valuable, leadership is not investing enough resources to create significant change. In Culture Amp's survey, 81% of DEI practitioners reported that they believe DEI initiatives benefit their organizations. Despite the obvious lack of resources to drive change, the overwhelming majority (85%) of respondents agreed that their organization is building a diverse and inclusive culture. There is a disconnect and a low level of investment, indicating that change is not likely to be substantial or sustainable without additional resource allocations.

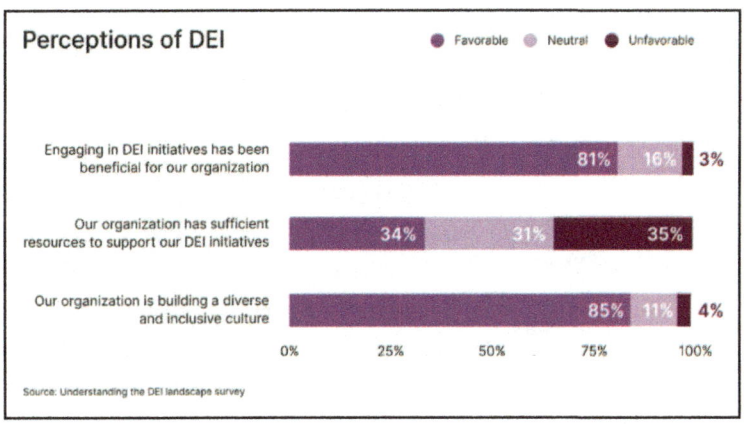

Source: Understanding the DEI Landscape Survey, Culture Amp's 2022 Workplace DEI Report

I recently led a discussion with a group of leaders in the marketing industry on the future of DEI. During the discussion, I asked the room of over 50 participants, "What is the one word you would use to describe the current state of DEI," the results were mildly encouraging but overwhelmingly sad. In fact, sad was one of the actual responses. I have good news - those surveyed also felt it was improving.

Look at the results presented below.

> **What is the one word you would use to describe the current state of Diversity, Equity & Inclusion?**
> Wordcloud Poll   62 responses   52 participants
>
> Inclusive, Overwhelming, Fragile, Subpar, Welcoming, Safety, Interesting, Talk, Progressing, Challenging, Intense, Ongoing, sad, burgeoning, Wellmeaning, Slow, **Improving**, Growing, Stagnant, Trendy, Trending, growth, Jeopardize, Progress, Hard, Misunderstood, Unorganized, Worthwhile, Under fire, Losing interest, Fluctuating, Infancy, Struggling, Emerging

Source: 2023 Amplify A|E|C, The Future of DEI: The Next 50 Years - Live Poll

A plethora of organizations are investing in DEI staffing and practitioners. However, nearly 60% of companies reported not having any DEI. 40% of DEI practitioners said they are investing in the expertise needed to build successful equity and inclusion programs. Organizations that rely on people to execute their mission and achieve business goals must develop a DEI strategy that aligns their goals and objectives with the equitable and inclusive treatment of the workforce. As organizations embark on their DEI journey, they must have a framework to guide their efforts. The framework serves as a road map to the organizational and people management systems that should be implemented, changed, or eliminated as they strive toward sustainable DEI programming and practices. My framework has always been

"Just do it!" Unfortunately, that is not enough. And there goes the dilemma again.

When employing equity initiatives, here are some of the actual dilemmas that arise: (a) diverse applicant pool challenges, (b) cultural changes, (c) tokenism, and (d) inability to retain talent to start, just to name a few.

Then, there is the dilemma that occurs when addressing the dilemma. The damage and destruction caused when the band-aids are ripped off, and well-meaning DEI activists get a glimpse behind the veil.

I start with Black women because I am one. I genuinely believe that if solutions can be found for us, often the most discriminated group in the world, solutions can be found for all. The fact is Black women constantly face multiple forms of discrimination in the world and the workplace, especially racial and gender-based discrimination. We typically experience unequal pay, limited career advancement opportunities, and microaggressions from our colleagues and superiors. This often leads to a lack of representation and visibility in leadership positions and a lack of support for our professional development.

Black women are more than often subject to stereotypes, such as being seen as aggressive or confrontational, which may impact performance evaluations and opportunities for promotion. Additionally, Black women may be subject to racial harassment, including racial slurs and negative comments, which creates a hostile work environment and leads to decreased job satisfaction and increased stress levels.

The women of color in the workplace are consistently beaten down and harassed yet we rise. To address this issue, at the minimum, companies must prioritize diversity and inclusion in their hiring and promotion practices, provide anti-discrimination training for employees, and establish a zero-tolerance policy for harassment and discrimination.

Additionally, we must be empowered to speak out against discrimination and advocate for ourselves in the workplace. Tia Tyree, a professor at Howard University, described *misogynoir* as contempt, dislike, or mistreatment of Black women. Tyree, whose research focuses on representations of Black women in mass media, social media, and hip-hop culture, emphasized that misogynoir has been part of the Black female experience in the United States for centuries.

The concept of *quiet quitting*, which refers to employees who stop going above and beyond their job requirements and instead focus solely on fulfilling their assigned tasks, gained attention in the media and social platforms even before the COVID-19 pandemic. The topic created controversy within the business community as some organizations viewed it as a decline in dedication. From my perspective as a member of the marginalized group, quiet quitting is not about slacking off, but rather shifting towards a focus on prioritizing work-life balance or what I term as work-life integration. I have often thought of quiet quitting as a needed shift from the plantation mentality of working our fingers to the bone in the hopes of fair or equitable pay and treatment someday. Let us remember that one of the goals of plantations was to master the art of turning human bodies into machines. But we will get to that and the myth of meritocracy later.

Quiet quitting was the predecessor to the Great Resignation of 2020 and 2021. This time, the workers did not just coast at their jobs – they acted on their personal and professional ambitions and resigned in droves. This led to an empowering period for workers nationwide who were finally ready to have a healthy work-life integration, ask for increased compensation, and enjoy more flexibility. Fast forward to today: 2023 is bringing a new workplace phenomenon, but this time, businesses are calling the shots with *quiet hiring*. According to CNBC, quiet hiring is when a company hires temporary workers or contractors to fill permanent positions or asks existing employees to fill in-demand roles and acquire new responsibilities without increasing compensation.

Essentially, quiet hiring is how companies deal with significant labor shortages without increasing wages or benefits for workers. So, how does this new phenomenon affect DEI, and why should businesses be cautious about the consequences of quiet hiring?

Most companies with DEI training on workplace bias, cultural sensitivity, and building a culture of belonging, offer that training to full-time employees–not temporary workers. As more and more businesses use contractors, freelancers, and non-employee labor, those workers are often left out of mandatory DEI training. This can cause companies with good intentions for DEI to lose track of their progress and implementation across all departments. When one full-time employee is tasked to do bias training and a newly hired contractor is not, it creates inconsistency for DEI in the workplace. With contract laborers taking up more roles within organizations, the lasting results of missed or skipped DEI training for temporary workers may cause a gap in progress that is yet to be seen.

Quiet hiring may widen pay and benefits gaps. Some businesses have stopped hiring because of rising demand for employee wages and a recession looming. Hiring temporary workers or asking existing employees to take on new roles without additional compensation will inevitably lead to a widening pay gap. This gap will exist both between contractors and employees and among employees in stable positions versus those in newly reassigned roles.

With women, minorities, and immigrants already experiencing significant pay gaps, hiring those same workers temporarily or asking existing workers to work harder without increased compensation, makes the DEI goal to close the wage gap much further out of reach. In fact, asking employees to do more work for the same pay could even be considered wage theft.

Additionally, 1099 contractors and temporary workers typically do not receive the full benefits packages usually afforded to full-time employees, like paid time off, parental leave, or equity stakes. Thus, creating an even more considerable disadvantage for temporary workers performing full-time work without full-time benefits.

Quiet hiring may increase burnout among workers. Burnout is increased when there is no potential for paid time off for temporary workers and no increase in pay for existing employees. In addition, burnout is exacerbated when workers cannot find work-life integration, or get the downtime needed to recover from the heavy demands of work. Inevitably, burnout is the result when employers do not compensate workers for additional responsibilities.

In DEI, we advocate for businesses to promote more significant work-life integration opportunities to lower or mitigate the effects of burnout. I often advise companies to be generous with benefits like paid time off, parental leave, and bereavement. Also, I advise employers to have greater respect for the boundaries employees set around their private time. Whether a worker is temporary or full-time, having the space to rest, relax, and return to work feeling rejuvenated should not be rare or the exception. It should be the standard.

One upside to quiet hiring is that international candidates may be given more opportunities for professional advancement than ever before. In industries like healthcare, where a labor shortage has been prevalent since the pandemic began, skilled workers from overseas are now filling roles that have long been in demand but have remained vacant.

Quiet hiring should not derail your DEI initiatives when policies and practices are applied evenly among temporary and full-time workers. If your company chooses to hire temporary workers in this current economic climate, be mindful of what opportunities temporary workers are afforded or deprived of. Are they being included in DEI training like their full-time counterparts? Your organization should include temporary workers in the typical employee training and protocols to ensure they are not left behind economically, psychologically, or professionally.

For current employees being asked to do more, leaders should strive to compensate those employees fairly for their increased responsibilities or provide other benefits like additional paid time off or longer parental leave. It is important to find ways to show existing employees that your organization cares about their well-being and that you want them to experience increased workplace satisfaction.

Organizations are rapidly filling vacancies. However, placing DEI at the forefront of training and onboarding can keep initiatives on track. In fact, organizations can ensure they maintain their DEI goals during transitions in employee-employer relations by implementing strategies that include leadership commitment. Having leadership committed to DEI goals communicates this commitment to all levels of the organization.

One of my favorite quotes is from the movie *Remember the Titans*. In this famous scene, when the team's leader questions the player, he chirps back, "Attitude Reflects Leadership!" Nothing is more accurate when attempting to lead DEI initiatives. Leaders should exemplify inclusive behaviors and prioritize diversity and equity in decision-making.

Other strategies to keep DEI at the forefront and to develop a strong DEI initiative include a commitment to continuous education. By providing ongoing DEI training to employees at all levels, you will also assist in maintaining awareness and understanding of the importance of diversity and inclusion, fostering a culture that values these principles. Be sure to conduct regular assessments of your DEI initiatives to measure progress and identify areas for improvement. Measurements can include surveys, focus groups, and other feedback mechanisms to gauge employee experiences and perceptions. If your organization cannot commit to these activities, it is a sign of their readiness and not your abilities.

Inclusive policies that ensure that diversity and equity considerations are embedded in the day-to-day operations and decision-making processes of the organization should go hand in hand with the company's commitment to DEI. Moreover, there should be consistent consideration to integrate DEI with the business strategy while making diversity and inclusion integral to the organization's mission and objectives. The fact is that DEI is not just the responsibility of the DEI person or employee resource group (ERG) leaders. When these activities occur, organizations can navigate transitions in employee-employer relations, and the efforts are more likely to be sustained during transitions.

THE GLASS CEILING AND THE STICKY FLOOR.

I first heard the term *sticky floor* from Niani Tolbert. Kudos to her work within her organization, Hire Black. She created this company because Black women make 50 cents to every dollar a White man makes. Black women lose over $900,000 in income over a 40-year career span due to pay inequities. The persistence of inequities is compounded by the Black women's penalty and the motherhood penalty, the latter imposing an additional 15–20% penalty on income due to the challenges faced by mothers. Together, these issues contribute to the concept of the sticky floor.

The *glass ceiling* refers to an invisible barrier that prevents certain groups, particularly women and minorities, from advancing to higher positions in the workplace despite their qualifications and abilities. On the other hand, the sticky floor concept refers to the phenomenon where individuals from disadvantaged backgrounds struggle to climb the career ladder due to various barriers– such as limited access to education, lack of opportunities, and social inequalities. The glass ceiling focuses on obstacles preventing upward mobility, particularly for marginalized groups, while the sticky floor emphasizes the challenges individuals face at the bottom of the socioeconomic ladder.

As we continue to define concepts that are often puzzling, let us look at another example from an employee that I will call Kelsi. Kelsi struggled throughout her career because she had a strong Southern accent. Her mother had a strong Southern accent, her grandmother also had a strong Southern accent, and so on. As brilliant as Kelsi was, she was often overlooked due to the perception and bias that individuals with a Southern accent are not as intelligent. Kelsi would usually be considered not ready for promotion. She seldom received serious consideration and was told that others might feel uneasy around her or struggle to understand her, primarily due to her accent and various baseless reasons.

Recognizing that accents or dialects have no bearing on a person's intelligence or capabilities is essential. Accents are simply variations in pronunciation and speech patterns that develop based on geographic, cultural, and linguistic factors. It is important to note that intelligence is a complex trait encompassing a range of cognitive abilities, problem-solving skills, and knowledge. Someone's accent or regional dialect cannot accurately determine or predict intelligence.

Stereotyping individuals based on their accents is unfair and perpetuates harmful biases. In Kelsi's case, her vernacular overshadowed her talent.

In contrast, there are countless examples of individuals with prominent Southern accents who were taken very seriously and some made it to the highest elected office of the United States of America: former Presidents Jimmy Carter, Bill Clinton, and George W. Bush – to name a few. Their status as White males availed them a privilege not offered to most minorities, especially minority women.

It is crucial to embrace diversity and recognize the value that different accents, dialects, and cultures bring to our society. Intelligence is not confined to any particular accent, region, or culture. It is present in individuals from all social classes, regardless of their way of speaking.

Next, is the example of Dawn. I met Dawn, a melanated woman who sported an elegant bald head that screamed confidence, at a conference. She told me she was hired to be the head of DEI for her organization - the only DEI person to support 60,000 employees. She seemed hopeful and confident; I, however, was not. I instantly recognized her situation as a clear example of how an organization can take advantage of a willing Black woman who is committed to making a change; even at the cost of extorting her. This would be unheard of in most industry circles. In fact, monopolizing compassion and commitment to our communities is one of the ultimate forms of aggression and hurt.

Then there are the eloquent, confident, and influential Black men. In my HR experience, these men have had a slim chance of success in corporate America. Black men face several challenges in corporate America, which can hinder their career progression and limit their opportunities for success. Some key challenges Black men encounter include limited representation and mentor imitation. Black men are typically underrepresented in leadership positions within corporations. This lack of representation can result in a need for more role models and mentors who can understand and advocate for their unique experiences and perspectives.

Black men often face implicit bias and negative stereotypes in corporate environments, which can significantly impact their professional experiences. These biases not only influence how they are perceived within the workplace but also affect the evaluation processes and opportunities for career advancement. The pervasive nature of these biases underscores the importance of fostering inclusive environments that recognize and challenge stereotypes, ensuring equitable opportunities for Black men to thrive and progress in their careers. Stereotypes such as being aggressive, unprofessional, or lacking competence can create additional barriers to career growth. Organizations must actively promote diversity, equity, and inclusion initiatives to address and mitigate these biases, fostering a workplace culture that values the unique contributions of individuals irrespective of their racial background.

Stereotypes such as being aggressive, unprofessional, or lacking competence can create additional barriers to career growth. Black men frequently encounter direct discrimination and racial bias in the workplace. They may experience unfair treatment in hiring, promotion, salary, and assignments based on their race rather than their qualifications or performance. This can result in lower job satisfaction, limited career progression, and a hostile work environment.

Building solid networks is crucial for career advancement. However, Black men may face challenges in accessing networking opportunities due to exclusionary practices, unconscious bias, and a lack of diverse professional circles.

These challenges can limit access to mentors, sponsors, and valuable connections that can facilitate career growth.

The majority often seem to have more abundant opportunities, with many hires originating from connections within the desired company or through relationships with individuals linked to the organization. This suggests that these opportunities extend beyond the standard channels of regular recruitment and hiring practices.

Black men often encounter microaggressions at a debilitating level. Microaggressions are subtle, usually unintentional, acts or comments that communicate hostility or derogatory assumptions about race or ethnicity. These microaggressions can create an uncomfortable and unwelcoming work environment, negatively impacting morale, productivity, and overall well-being.

Black men may face pressure to conform to certain stereotypes or suppress aspects of their authentic selves to fit into the dominant corporate culture. This emotional labor can be exhausting and hinder their ability to fully express their true identities, perspectives, and talents. Black men may also face challenges related to their intersectional identities. Factors such as age, sexual orientation, disability, or socioeconomic background can compound the discrimination and obstacles they encounter in corporate America.

It is important to note that these challenges are not experienced uniformly by all Black men in corporate America. The extent of these obstacles can vary based on industry, company culture, individual skills, and personal experiences. Addressing these challenges involves promoting diversity and inclusion initiatives, fostering equitable practices, creating supportive networks, and raising awareness about unconscious bias and racial disparities.

On the other side of these aggressions are the majority trying to understand it all. To them, DEI is just another affirmative action program, another way to enable those who make excuses, a headache, and a waste of time. Recently, a

White, heterosexual friend of mine called upset and confused. He shared that he was being fired for making a derogatory comment to a Black male colleague. He described how his colleague thought that he commented on the type of car another Black customer was driving. My friend was adamant about the fact that he did not say anything about the Black man's car and that he knew he would not have said anything and vehemently denied doing anything wrong. He called me seeking empathy and understanding because he knew he and I were friends.

All the while, I could visualize him making a face and presenting body language that expressed surprise when he saw this Black man pull up in his car. In my imagination, it was a beautifully detailed luxury BMW, the type of car that has warranted stares and disapproving glances when Black and Brown bodies sit in it. My friend was absolutely clueless and could not understand how his behavior towards another colleague who just happened to be Black could have been offensive. All the while, I knew he was not beyond this type of judgmental behavior due to various reasons, one being race and other his current socioeconomic position that would cause him to look sideways at someone who may have been doing better than him—especially a Black man.

In my attempt to empathize, I did feel empathy for his inability to understand how slights happen ever so easily, and that it is only when it is brought to our attention that we are aware that it has happened. However, I knew that his comments towards his colleague regarding the type of car he drove, and his body language were probably just enough to add injury to many years of insults that my friend had nothing to do with.

Trust me, I get it. I have done it, and once again, here lies our dilemma. To learn how to manage microaggressions, they must occur. For example, after visiting the home of one of my close friends and colleagues, I was impressed with her interior decoration. The beautiful muted yellow and orange colors, the bright, airy feel of the room, the elegant furniture. My immediate response was, "Your home is so Italian!" After a beautiful afternoon, I thought how grateful I was to have a friend of such means and good taste. She called me the next day, sounding hurt and sad.

She asked, "What did you mean by my home was so Italian?" She described how offended she was and thought I meant I was trying to say her house was dirty or unkept, an unfortunate stereotype Italian Americans faced during the early years after arriving in America. I never forget how she bought it home for me by asking, "How would you feel if I said your home is so Black?" We all have lots of lessons to learn and re-learn.

No one is exempt from committing macro and microaggressions, regardless of how you identify.

1
THE POWER OF A WORD

Accept one another, then, just as Christ accepted you, in order to bring praise to God. – Romans 15:7 NIV

O people, we created you from the same male and female and rendered you distinct peoples and tribes that you may recognize one another. The best among you in the sight of GOD is the most righteous. GOD is Omniscient, Cognizant. – Quran 49:13

You shall not render an unfair decision; do not favor the poor nor show deference to the rich; judge your fellow fairly. – Lev. 19:15

One of the most read phrases in one of the most read books – the Bible –states in the Book of John 1:1, "In the beginning (of creation) was the Word." Words have power. The expression "words have power" reflects the belief that the words we use can profoundly impact ourselves and others. Words are the primary means of human communication. They allow us to convey our thoughts, feelings, and ideas to others. How we express ourselves through words can influence how others perceive us and understand our message or intent. Words can evoke strong emotions in people. They have the power to inspire, motivate, uplift, and comfort. Conversely, they can also hurt, insult, and demoralize. The choice of words can significantly influence the emotional state of individuals and shape their experiences.

Words have the power to persuade and influence others. Effective communication can change people's opinions, attitudes, and behaviors. Skillful use of language can sway public opinion, negotiate agreements, and inspire collective action. Words let us express our thoughts, beliefs, values, and identity. They shape our self-image and help us connect with others who share similar ideas. Our choice of words can reflect our personality, culture, and worldview. Therefore, recognizing and respecting the power of words and using them responsibly is vital.

How we communicate can have a lasting impact on ourselves and those around us. Choosing our words carefully, considering their potential effects, and using them to uplift, inspire, and connect can lead to more positive and meaningful interactions as we tackle inclusion and equity. Let us look at a few definitions that have created emotionally charged and heated conversations in DEI.

ABLEISM

According to the Merriam-Webster dictionary, ableism is discrimination or prejudice against individuals with disabilities. It is a term used to describe discrimination, prejudice, or bias against individuals with disabilities. It refers to the systemic and societal attitudes, beliefs, and practices that devalue and marginalize people with disabilities, often by assuming that able-bodied individuals are superior in some way. Ableism encompasses discriminatory actions, policies, or behaviors that disadvantage or exclude individuals with disabilities. This can manifest in various forms, such as unequal access to employment, education, healthcare, transportation, or public spaces.

These stereotypes may include assuming that individuals with disabilities are less capable, less intelligent, or less valuable than those without disabilities. Since ableism often results in the design of environments, products, and services that do not consider the needs of individuals with disabilities, significant barriers to participation in society are the result. Organizations and communities often miss this level of impact on diverse communities.

Ableism can lead to the assumption that individuals with disabilities are inherently dependent on others rather than recognizing their autonomy and abilities. This assumption can limit opportunities for independence and self-determination. In addition, ableism can result in the social exclusion and stigmatization of people with disabilities, making it challenging for them to fully participate in various aspects of life and society.

When institutions or individuals do not provide reasonable accommodations for people with disabilities, it is a manifestation of ableism. Accommodations can include accessible facilities, communication aids, or flexible work arrangements.

It is important to point out that people with disabilities often face higher rates of unemployment and underemployment, which can lead to economic disparities. Ableism can contribute to these disparities by limiting job opportunities and workplace discrimination. Ableism can intersect with other forms of discrimination, such as racism, sexism, or homophobia, leading to unique challenges for individuals who belong to multiple marginalized groups.

Challenging ableism involves advocating for equal rights, accessibility, and inclusion for people with disabilities, as well as raising awareness about the harmful effects of ableist attitudes and practices. Promoting disability rights, fostering understanding, and actively working to eliminate ableism are essential steps toward creating a more equitable and inclusive society for all.

BELONGING

According to the Cambridge Dictionary, the definition of belonging is a feeling of being happy or comfortable as part of a particular group and having a good relationship with the other members of the group because they welcome and accept you. Another interesting take on belonging is having the right personal or social qualities to be a member of a particular group.

Belonging is an emotional state that is the goal of DEI efforts. Your organization's inclusive processes are there to make everyone feel welcome. For someone to feel genuinely welcome, they need to feel welcome exactly as they are. They should not have to consciously (or unconsciously, for that matter) check a part of themselves at the door.

Belonging is a universal human need, ranked third on Abraham Maslow's hierarchy of needs which he developed in 1943. The need for affiliation and belonging is still a legitimate and dependable predictor for success today. Subsequently, research shows that when we experience feelings of acceptance, it positively affects the prefrontal cortex of our brain.

Belonging was one of the most critical human capital issues at the top of the 2021 Global Human Capital Trends survey. Nearly 79% of survey respondents said that fostering a sense of belonging in the workforce was essential to their organization's success in the next twelve to eighteen months, and 93% agreed that belonging drives organizational performance.

By creating workplace cultures that foster morale and camaraderie, we can also impact lives outside of work. Companies need to focus on their values and decision-making processes to build this kind of culture. The good news is that a sense of belonging can be increased by manifesting behaviors that foster intentional inclusion.

Simply put, belonging is in the eye of the beholder. In a perfect world, everyone feels welcome. To feel genuinely welcome involves feeling accepted exactly as you are. This applies in organizations where employees should not have to check a piece of themselves at the door.

BIASES

There are numerous definitions of bias and they all can lead to unintended consequences. According to the American Heritage Dictionary, bias is defined as a preference or an inclination, especially one that inhibits impartial judgment.

What has become difficult to solve is how we dismantle bias every day. Biases are difficult to manage because our brains are programmed to scan for race, gender, and age within one second of encountering another person. Note to DEI practitioners - I have shared this statement while working for organizations and was guided to say that our brains *may* be programmed to scan for race. No, our brains are programmed, and it is not a negative thing or a judgment, it just is.

Research indicates that human beings innately perceive differences in others as a threat due to an evolutionary requirement in our brains. We have a fundamental need to discern an in-group and out-group, them from us. Computing differences takes only a fraction of a second and is the prerequisite for bias, stereotypes, and prejudices. A network of neural structures in multiple regions of our brains plays a role in how we perceive social threats.

According to researcher, Dr. Anna Nikki Douglas, biases are formed from our socialization practices and experiences. Our fight or flight responses are innate characteristics and only through socialization and organization of our cognitive schemas can we decide which option is best.

Short version, we all have bias. Period.

COLORISM

Colorism is a form of discrimination or prejudice based on the shade of someone's skin color, with lighter skin tones often being favored over darker ones. This bias can occur within the same racial or ethnic group. Colorism often results in unfair treatment and opportunities based on skin color rather than individual merit or abilities. As a lighter-skinned individual, I am aware that I have received preferential treatment in education, employment, and social interactions. I see and sense the responses of my skin color instantly when I walk into a room.

Among marginalized people, the closer we have been to the dominant caste in hair, skin color, and facial features, the higher we rank on the scale. Especially troubling in the United States are colorism and caste. Colorism reinforces harmful stereotypes about beauty, intelligence, and success being associated with lighter skin tones. This perpetuates unrealistic and damaging standards of beauty, contributing to low self-esteem and negative self-perception among those with darker skin. Individuals who experience colorism may suffer from psychological distress, including anxiety, depression, and low self-esteem. Constant exposure to biased attitudes and discrimination can lead to a negative impact on mental health.

I have seen colorism create division and tension within communities and individuals being pitted against each other based on their skin color. In my own family, I can remember comments being made expressing disappointment when a child was born with darker skin. I grew up to a myriad of comments about dark and ashy skin, nappy "Brillo" pad hair, and just overall disdain and sadness if someone in our family was of a darker complexion. On the other side, I received kindness, hugs, and special attention due to my lighter skin and "pretty" complexion.

This internal strife weakens community solidarity and can hinder progress towards common goals. Colorism often has deep historical roots, stemming from colonialism, slavery, and other forms of oppression.

Colorism is often intertwined with broader issues of systemic racism and discrimination. By perpetuating unequal treatment based on skin color, it contributes to and reinforces existing patterns of inequality. The focus on skin color can affect personal relationships, including romantic partnerships and family dynamics. Addressing colorism involves challenging and changing societal attitudes, promoting inclusivity, and fostering a greater appreciation for diversity.

CAPITALISM

It is essential to consider the intersectionality of race, gender, and other identities when assessing the impact of capitalism on minorities. Some minority groups, such as Black women or transgender individuals, face compounded discrimination, experiencing distinct challenges within capitalist systems. It is important to note that these effects are not inherent to capitalism itself but rather reflections of how capitalism has operated within a specific historical and social context. Efforts to address these disparities often involve policy interventions, such as affirmative action, anti-discrimination laws, and targeted support for minority-owned businesses.

The concept of *whiteness* was constructed as a rationalization and legitimation for the othering and dehumanization of non-Europeans. Capitalism's growth depended on the trade of enslaved people, making it challenging to separate capitalism from racism. In short, capitalism's growth has relied on racism and cannot be separated from it.

Discriminatory practices where financial institutions deny loans or insurance to specific neighborhoods based on racial composition, have limited minority communities' access to housing and credit. Employment discrimination and wage disparities have also been observed, with minorities facing lower wages and reduced opportunities for career advancement.

Historically, capitalism has exploited minority labor, both domestically and internationally. In the United States, Black people and other minorities have often been subject to unfair labor practices, such as lower wages, hazardous working conditions, and limited benefits. Additionally, minority workers have frequently been overrepresented in low-wage and precarious jobs.

Capitalism has offered opportunities for minority entrepreneurship and wealth creation. Despite significant obstacles, some of us have successfully defied the odds, established businesses, and achieved economic success. However, access to capital and resources necessary for entrepreneurial ventures have often been limited for minorities, perpetuating disparities.

Capitalism's consumer-driven nature has led to targeted marketing and advertising, which can sometimes reinforce stereotypes and exploit minority communities. Companies have been known to use cultural symbols or misrepresent minority cultures for commercial gain, perpetuating harmful narratives. As an illustration, the cotton cultivated by enslaved individuals was transported to factories in England and the Northern regions of America. In these factories, predominantly White laborers transformed the raw material into cloth and fashioned clothing.

The concept of *race* was strategically employed as a means to placate White workers, affording them a marginal sense of superiority over the enslaved individuals in the Southern states. Lyndon Johnson shared, "If you can convince the lowest White man he is better than the best-colored man, he will not notice you are picking his pocket. Give him somebody to look down on, and he will empty his pockets for you."

The deliberate actions of our White-dominated government, through housing, zoning, and banking policies, actively contribute to and perpetuate these disparities. These policies made it substantially more challenging for Black individuals to secure a loan at fair rates or acquire property beyond areas designated as ghettos.

In the Netflix show *1619*, Nicole Hannah addressed capitalism and how it is deeply aligned with the overall treatment of humans. Hannah compared the plantation workers and pickers to the pickers at a well-known distribution company. She compared picking hundreds of bales of cotton to workers picking hundreds of packages for the distribution company. Recently, I learned firsthand the effects of unfair treatment and hypocrisy from the same company.

My neurodiverse niece was a picker at the company until she was terminated because of her inability to keep up with the pace. The company spouts DEI for neurodiversity; however, according to my niece, they did not offer her an accommodation and stayed focused solely on her ability to produce. This behavior stems from and is rooted in capitalism. This is just one of many examples of the dilemma. To compound that dilemma is our dependency on these companies despite their inequitable business practices. The fact is success in corporate America is dependent on the exploitation of labor.

The Rev. Dr. Martin Luther King, Jr. critiqued capitalism and addressed the economic disparities African Americans faced. He criticized the unequal distribution of wealth in society. One of his notable quotes on economic justice is, "Capitalism does not permit an even flow of economic resources. With this system, a small privileged few are rich beyond conscience, and almost all others are doomed to be poor at some level."

King had strong views on capitalism and how it was built. In fact, King stated in his 1967, The Three Evils Speech, "Again we have deluded ourselves into believing the myth that capitalism grew and prospered out of the Protestant ethic of hard work and sacrifices. Capitalism was built on the exploitation of Black slaves and continues to thrive on the exploitation of the poor, both Black and White, both here and abroad."

CULTURAL FIT

Harvard Business Review defines cultural fit as the likelihood that someone will reflect and/or be able to adapt to the core beliefs, attitudes, and behaviors that make up your organization. A good cultural fit is when employees' beliefs and behaviors align with their employer's core values and company culture. While the concept of cultural fit aligns the employees with the desired work culture, we must also consider the cultural requirements the organization promotes. Does the organization promote Eurocentric values or encourage Eurocentric standards of dress, communication, and accent? The problem occurs when the term cultural fit is used far more often as a reason not to hire someone. In the paradox of the term and use of the word cultural fit, hiring managers use the concept of cultural fit to allow a firm to hire people who can quickly adapt to their organizational norms.

One study viewed the cultural fit strategies of 55 organizations and showed that 9 out of 10 recruiters passed over applicants because they needed to match the company's current culture. With a clearly defined culture and interview process, the hiring criteria of cultural fit can become very subjective, causing an impediment to DEI initiatives. For example, as an HR practitioner, I have witnessed multiple situations where the hiring manager openly shared that a candidate would not be a good cultural fit which could only be assumed to be based on their ethnicity, race, or gender. In those cases, it was clear the wrong attributes were used as a factor for cultural fit rather than their skills, abilities, or talents.

When recruiters focus on the required set of corporate values aligning with the potential candidate rather than the personal cultural characteristics of the candidate, organizations can achieve a skills-based, heterogeneous staff. If organizations continue to hire people who are just like existing employees, then they will misuse the term cultural fit as an attempt to disguise discrimination against underrepresented groups. They would only succeed in creating a homogeneous workplace lacking diverse perspectives, ideas, and creativity.

DIVERSITY

Diversity and inclusion are not synonymous terms. We increasingly hear diversity and inclusion in conversations regarding equality and social justice. These two concepts are often paired like peanut butter and jelly. However, this comparison needs to be more accurate. In order to deal with the multiple dilemmas that surround diversity, understanding the distinction between diversity and inclusion is crucial.

Let us explore the different meanings of the two words from a practical point of view.

Diversity is a representation of types of people, including gender, race, ability, religion, age, sexual orientation, socioeconomic status, political affiliation, marital status, and ability levels. Separate from dimensions of diversity, inclusion implies an atmosphere where everyone has an equal chance to participate in the decision-making process and have equal opportunities for success. Inclusion requires practices and policies to welcome and treat people with diverse backgrounds equally. Diversity is most meaningful when met with inclusive practices.

When I started my work in diversity, my first encounters were laced with warnings about being careful when using the word diversity. To my surprise, the word diversity held a negative connotation with many people. I was met with comments that the word diversity makes leaders look bad. Another popular sentiment was that the word diversity was polarizing. And that the word diversity should be replaced with a word that people can relate to and accept if they want to be successful. My response was, "huh?" and "No."

Diversity involves recognizing, valuing, and appreciating people's unique characteristics, perspectives, backgrounds, and identities based on race, ethnicity, gender, sexual orientation, age, religion, socioeconomic status, disability, and more. In the context of diversity, the emphasis is on embracing and celebrating differences rather than seeking uniformity.

Diversity promotes inclusivity and recognizes that each person has their own experiences, viewpoints, and contributions to offer. It recognizes that a diverse group can bring various perspectives, talents, and skills, leading to better decision-making, innovation, creativity, and societal progress. Promoting diversity involves creating an environment that respects and values individual differences, providing equal opportunities for all, and ensuring everyone has a voice and is treated fairly and with dignity. It is an ongoing process that requires open-mindedness, empathy, and a commitment to fostering inclusivity and equality. Now, to inclusion.

To comprehend inclusion, an exploration of exclusion and its historical context globally, beyond America, is essential. Examining Eastern and Western beliefs is crucial, as they contribute to addressing issues of exclusion. The concepts of enslavement, colonization, uplift suasion, and systemic racism only scratch the surface of the complexities inherent in understanding the phenomenon of exclusion.

Inclusion refers to the practice of creating an environment or society that embraces and values diversity. It involves actively seeking to ensure that individuals of different backgrounds, perspectives, abilities, and identities feel welcomed, respected, and fully engaged.

Inclusion goes beyond mere tolerance; it strives for the active participation and contribution of everyone, fostering a sense of belonging and equality. In an inclusive setting, people are recognized and appreciated for their unique qualities, and efforts are made to remove barriers that might otherwise lead to exclusion or discrimination. The goal of inclusion is to create a culture where diversity is celebrated, and each individual feels empowered to thrive and contribute to the collective success of the community or organization. Inclusion is intentional. Inclusion is a verb that evokes action. To be inclusive, you must do something.

EQUITY & EQUALITY

Equality is not asking people to pull themselves up by their bootstraps but making sure everyone has boots on. Equity is making sure everyone's boots fit! There are various images of equality versus equity. We can refer to the illustration of various types of people of all different sizes riding the same size bicycle. In fact, one of these people is in a wheelchair and cannot get on the bike provided. The ideal picture is of the same group of people with various sizes of bicycles. Bicycles that are custom fit to each person's needs – that's equity.

Bicycle Image. Courtesy of Robert Wood Johnson Foundation

There is a myth that making things equal is somehow cheating. Ironically, marginalized groups are accused of cheating the system, when groups of privilege have received a head start in the race. Head starts have defined our country.

Redlining stands out as a particularly insidious example of a head start for the majority class, constituting an egregious abuse of power and exclusion. The practice, along with the resulting racial segregation and discrimination against minority populations, predates the specific process termed redlining in the United States. This process commenced with the National Housing Act of 1934 and the concurrent establishment of the Federal Housing Administration.

Implementing this federal policy accelerated the decay and isolation of minority inner-city neighborhoods by withholding mortgage capital. This made it even more difficult for neighborhoods to attract and retain families able to purchase homes. The discriminatory assumptions in redlining exacerbated residential racial segregation and urban decay in the United States. The effects of redlining can be seen today throughout the United States with almost near-accurate precision between the haves and the have-nots.

The impact of redlining has directly affected my family, making it challenging for us to attain property and escape poverty. In 2011, we received a check from Countrywide Home Loans, the same institution that had previously put us through numerous hurdles to secure a mortgage. Throughout the years, we consistently sensed unequal treatment, facing more frequent loan denials and higher interest rates, all attributed to our race. The $25.00 check we received from the $33 million settlement served as confirmation of our suspicions.

The level of sensitivity that occurs when we start talking about diversity, equity, and equality has always brought with it certain shocking factors. For example, while conducting a company presentation, one of the first things pointed out was a sense that equity was, in and of itself, not fair for all parties.

Soapbox Image. Courtesy of Interaction Institute for Social Change. Retrieved from https://interactioninstitute.org/illustrating-equality-vs-equity/.

For instance, the image of the bicyclists somehow goes over more favorably with an audience than those sad persons standing on the soap boxes. Why? First, how do we know they are sad if we cannot see their faces? They are sad because they do not have tickets to the game, they have not been invited, and a huge fence and some raggedy boxes are blocking them from getting into the game.

At first glance, the image of the soapboxes make perfect sense. However, it has created numerous disagreements when shared with various audiences. Where some see equity, others see favoritism. Others see not receiving fair treatment because of the color of their skin, and others see people who need to pull themselves up by their bootstraps, just like them.

During the numerous equity presentations, I have led and attended, the shorter person in the illustration has been blamed for the lack of equity. Consider this: the shortest boy is positioned as the problem since he requires multiple boxes to see over the fence. He is considered "less" than the others. The shortest boy is — by sheer presentation alone — not whole, not "normal," especially compared to the tallest boy. And because he is shorter, he is seen as the problem; he needs more help. He is, in fact, needy.

The reality is that the problem lies within the system. The boxes would not be required if the actual ground, the system, was level. Then, there is the fence; people often ask, *why can't we just remove the whole fence?* And *why can't those people behind the fence work hard and get tickets like everyone else, just like my grandparents when they walked to school barefoot in the snow?*

Overall, this image is a glaring and unsettling visual representation of the stealthy systemic issues that have created overall barriers to equity and justice for all. This image effectively illustrates the significant contrast between equality and equity, conveying that treating everyone equally does not result in fairness. It has helped people understand that equal treatment can sometimes reinforce and rationalize racial hierarchies.

In summary, equality aims to treat everyone the same – regardless of their circumstances, while equity recognizes the unique needs of individuals and seeks to provide resources and opportunities that cater to those differences. The bicycle analogy highlights the importance of considering individual needs and circumstances to achieve true fairness and justice.

In 1987, as a young adult, I was invited to participate in an Equal Educational Opportunity Program (EEOP) at Kean College in New Jersey. I was unaware of the politics of EEOP; I only knew that college could be an opportunity and a safe haven for me from the chaos and dysfunction that came with having drug-addicted parents. My mom had broken our landlord's last straw (either not paying the rent or just making them angry for the final time), and she would be days away from being evicted. All I knew was I would not have a place to live, and the EEOP offered an opportunity to live on campus.

I enthusiastically accepted room and board in exchange for my education, an opportunity that exposed me to a different world on campus. Despite being considered a "D" student in high school, I found myself in a supportive setting with a college counselor that allowed me to excel. In this environment, I had equal opportunities compared to my White counterparts, including access to the same books, materials, resources, professors, and even nutrition. I learned proper study habits and other skills, often practicing until 3:00 am each morning to catch up. The EEOP program provided me with the chance to see what was possible and equipped me with the tools to make it possible. This is an example of equity, not a handout.

Later on, unbeknownst to me, my experience would be minimized during my time at the university. We became the "affirmative action" kids. Both Black and White professors would take one look at me and assume I would be trouble. This action was exclusion and segregation at its best. I kept my head down, did the work, and graduated Magna Cum Laude. Nothing was easy; nothing was given to me; I worked twice as hard to catch up, graduating within the top ten of my class with a 3.75 grade point average. I was exhausted, I was alienated, and I was not taken seriously. No matter how hard I worked, I could not understand how the trouble-maker persona remained the perception. I did not understand racism the way I know it now.

By recognizing and accommodating the varying needs of individuals, equity ensures fairness. It is important to note that equity does not mean treating everyone exactly the same but tailoring support and resources to account for different starting points and needs. It aims to address disparities and promote equal outcomes by acknowledging and rectifying historical and systemic injustices. Both equity and equality are essential concepts in discussions of fairness and justice. While equality emphasizes treating everyone equally, equity recognizes the need to address disparities and provide individuals with what they need to achieve equal opportunities and outcomes.

EEOC, EQUALITY & EQUITY

It has been said that the Equal Employment Opportunity (EEO) laws give everyone the same opportunity to thrive, while affirmative action actively supports those consistently deprived of fair and equal treatment. In the legal sense of the EEO definition, same chances or equal opportunity means that employers cannot use specific characteristics as reasons to hire or reject candidates or make other employment decisions; in other words, they cannot discriminate against those characteristics. In many countries, protected characteristics include:

Race/color
National origin/ethnicity
Religion
Age

Sex/gender/sexual orientation
Physical or mental disability

EEO does not guarantee that people of underrepresented groups will get hired. EEO regulations aim to ensure nobody will face rejection or difficulties because they are in a protected group. For example, under several EEO laws, you cannot reject a candidate simply because they are Jewish or Christian, African or Caucasian, or because they are pregnant. Similarly, you cannot advertise jobs asking for candidates of a certain age or promote men over women – you can only base this decision on each person's proven capabilities, performance, and other objective criteria rather than biases against protected groups.

If your company fails to comply with equal employment opportunity regulations, you may face complaints, lawsuits, and fines. There are also intangible costs associated with having a homogenous instead of a diverse workforce; there is an advantage of different perspectives and approaches to work.

United States regulations require some employers to file the EEO-1 report to track how EEO-compliant organizations are. Generally, if you have over 100 employees, or you are a federal contractor with more than 50 employees and a federal contract worth more than $50,000, you will need to file an EEO-1 report. EEO is giving everyone the same opportunity to thrive, while affirmative action actively supports those consistently deprived of fair and equal treatment. Affirmative action and diversity often need clarification. Affirmative action is numbers-oriented, aimed at changing the demographics within the organization. Managing diversity is behavioral, aimed at changing the organizational culture and developing skills and policies that get the best from everyone.

Creating equity within your workplace takes your commitment to diversity even further, by ensuring you have processes and programs in place that provide all employees with access to equitable opportunities for growth.

You need to know when and why your diverse recruits leave. Hence, the next step is analyzing retention patterns. HR should be able to see at what point in the career path minority exiting occurs. Tracking employee loss and its reasons is critical. Questions you should be able to answer:

- What inclusionary activities does your company engage in when hiring a new recruit?
- Are formal corporate activities and events planned to appeal to all employees and not just a few?
- Does your employee training on DEI include the importance of inclusion?
- Do you know if informal employee activities or events tend to be clique-ish and exclusionary?
- At what point do your diverse populations leave your organization?
- How many years have they been there? What departments are they in? Is there a pattern around when they quit?
- How do promotion rates differ by, for example, gender or ethnicity across your organization?
- Do minority members work longer in the same job than their non-minority counterparts?
- Is readiness for upward mobility viewed differently for different populations?

In addressing DEI, what you do not know can hurt you. Mercer reports that two in five employees plan to leave their company in the next twelve months, yet only one in four HR leaders use analytics to ascertain why they joined their organization in the first place.

It is highly recommended that organizations conduct a corporate-wide internal audit to determine what may be working today in policies and practices. Leaders need the tools to conduct an accurate assessment and the ability to understand and act on the results. Tech companies are finding DEI analytics and monitoring the second most significant product area following talent acquisition. More tools are available. Failure to use them to help realize your DEI initiatives may be at your peril. It also leaves open the door for other perilous issues.

EQUITY AND THE MEDIA

Americans have a fascination with celebrities. Ironically, the treatment of celebrities can provide additional insight into inclusion. Exploring the history of the treatment of celebrities of color in America further illustrates the issue of inclusion in America. I love Josephine Baker. She was a rebel with a strong cause, a trailblazer, and a force to be reckoned with, and America loved and hated her. Each time Baker returned to the United States, she found that many Americans resented her European success. In 1936, when she was lured back to New York to appear in the Ziegfeld Follies, billed below Fanny Brice, critics were brutal. Time magazine called her "a Negro wench … a slightly buck-toothed young Negro woman whose figure might be matched in any night-club show, and whose dancing and singing might be topped practically anywhere outside of Paris." Music has been an ultimate phenomenon, bringing together and uniting. As Little Richard, the innovator and originator of Rock and Roll, shared, "My music broke down segregation."

We can also learn from the treatment and views of Cassius Clay's evolution to Muhammad Ali. Oprah Winfrey's treatment and America's view of her beauty on her rise to success and status is a case study of the impact of media on DEI. In the early 2000s, media mogul Oprah Winfrey's influence extended beyond her talk show and into the lives of millions. Her story revolves around a significant moment when Oprah used her platform to challenge societal norms and grant individuals the freedom to embrace their natural beauty. At the time, natural hairstyles like braids, twists, and afros were often considered unprofessional or inappropriate in specific workplaces and social circles.

The prevailing beauty standards upheld Eurocentric ideals, leaving People of Color feeling pressured to conform to straightened or chemically altered hairstyles to be accepted. One memorable episode of Oprah's talk show took a stand against these discriminatory norms. During this episode, Oprah shared her experiences with hair and self-acceptance, recounting how she had struggled with her appearance early in her career. She spoke candidly about how society's beauty standards had influenced her choices and her journey towards embracing her natural self.

As part of the episode, Oprah welcomed a diverse panel of guests, including hairstylists, cultural critics, and everyday people who had faced discrimination due to their natural hairstyles. Their heartfelt stories shed light on the emotional toll of feeling pressured to conform and the liberation from embracing one's authentic self. Oprah then made a powerful declaration: she granted everyone in her audience and beyond permission to wear their hair in whatever way made them feel comfortable and confident. This declaration reverberated through the audience, prompting cheers and tears of relief.

The impact of Oprah's words extended beyond the episode. People nationwide felt empowered to proudly wear braids, twists, and other natural hairstyles without fearing judgment or backlash. This transformative moment challenged beauty standards and sparked a broader conversation about self-acceptance and embracing cultural identity.

Years later, Oprah's stance continues to be celebrated as a milestone in fighting against discriminatory beauty norms. Her courage to challenge societal expectations empowered countless individuals to reclaim their natural beauty and helped pave the way for more inclusive conversations around diversity and representation in various aspects of society. Oprah is just one example of how the entertainment industry plays a significant role in shaping the DEI conversation due to its broad reach, influence, and ability to reflect and impact societal attitudes.

The entertainment industry can shape public perception by showcasing diverse characters and stories on screen through representation. By depicting people from various backgrounds, cultures, races, genders, sexual orientations, and abilities, it normalizes diversity and contributes to a more inclusive narrative.

Diverse storytelling helps viewers connect with characters and experiences they might not encounter daily. This cultivates empathy, understanding, and acceptance as audiences are exposed to different perspectives and challenges marginalized groups face.

Through plots and narratives, the entertainment industry can address social issues such as racism, sexism, LGBTQ+ rights, and more. These storylines spark conversations and raise awareness, fostering a greater understanding of underrepresented communities' struggles.

High-profile productions embracing diversity and inclusivity set a standard for the entire industry. The success of diverse films, TV shows, and performances proves that audiences are receptive to inclusive content, encouraging more productions to follow suit. Casting actors from different backgrounds in roles that are not traditionally associated with those backgrounds challenges stereotypes and promotes authenticity. This conveys that talent is universal and not confined by one's identity.

Encouraging diversity in front of the camera and behind it (directors, writers, producers, crew members) ensures that diverse voices influence storytelling from conception to execution, resulting in more nuanced and accurate portrayals. Award ceremonies, though sometimes criticized for their lack of diversity, also spotlight outstanding achievements and contributions by individuals from underrepresented groups. Recognizing diverse talent can motivate others and inspire change.

The entertainment industry has the potential to push boundaries and challenge traditional norms, highlighting narratives that defy stereotypes and create opportunities for underrepresented voices to be heard. Documentaries, docuseries, and informative shows can educate audiences about different cultures, histories, and experiences, breaking down barriers of ignorance and fostering a more inclusive society. Production companies, studios, and entertainment conglomerates often have a social responsibility to advocate for diversity and inclusion within their content and workforce. Their actions can influence other industries to prioritize DEI efforts.

While the entertainment industry has made strides, work still needs to be done. As society becomes more conscious of the need for representation and inclusivity, the industry must continue to evolve, acknowledge its shortcomings, and actively create a more diverse and inclusive landscape that resonates with and empowers people from all levels of society.

Both Rev. Dr. Martin Luther King, Jr. and Malcolm X were subjected to significant challenges and adversity during their lifetimes, but they also garnered support and influence that helped begin to shape the course of the civil rights movement in the United States – all while being broadcast via television and radio. King was more widely recognized and celebrated for his nonviolent activism, while Malcolm X was seen as a more controversial figure and faced more significant opposition and scrutiny. We can also learn from our present state and the martyrs who have gained celebrity status for the wrong reasons. Martyrs such as Ahmaud Arbery were killed on February 23, 2020. Breonna Taylor was killed on March 13, 2020; Steven Demarco Taylor was killed on April 18, 2020; and George Floyd was killed on May 25, 2020.

Over the past 400 years, there have been many incidents in this country that did not receive national prominence. Each and every one of these deaths feels like a modern-day lynching. Reminding us of the race relations in our country and our world. Sadly, all of these instances and images remind me and my family to stay in our lane, stay in our homes, and behave in the workplace and outside, or we may suffer the same horrible fate we see played out in the media daily.

I recently experienced a distressing incident on the Nextdoor app that left me terrified. A fellow community member posted an image of a young Black man in a hoodie walking near a neighbor's property, urging caution among residents. The image captured the individual merely walking, yet the post implied potential danger. The sight immediately triggered concerns about my own two Black sons facing unwarranted scrutiny, harassment, or worse in our neighborhood.

Promptly, I responded to the post, advising against sharing vague, potentially misleading images that could fuel fear and suspicion toward Black individuals. I emphasized that the person in the photo could easily be my family member, highlighting the need for discretion when posting generic images and sharing information. My message conveyed a genuine concern about the risk of fostering an atmosphere of suspicion within our community. I immediately thought of Trayvon Martin, George Floyd, Michael Brown, and so many other Black bodies that have been killed by police for simply walking or being Black.

HOMOPHILY

Organizations have become cognizant of diversity and inclusion practices as our society becomes more diverse. However, organizations can find it challenging to go beyond compliance-driven requirements. Before advertising for employment positions, organizations should evaluate and modify their recruitment processes to attract diverse candidates. Often, organizations rely on internal references to find new employees.

Homophily is an inclination for people to have bonds with those who share similarities with them- this might explain why many candidates hired through internal referrals might belong to the same demographic as their current employees. This phenomenon has a direct, detrimental impact on diversity within the workplace. For example, consider a small business with 25 White male employees seeking to fill a position based on current employee referrals. What do you think are the chances that the new employee will also be a White male?

Another aspect of the job-recruitment process is job description wording. Does the wording discourage a specific demographic from applying? Certain terms in the description might imply the position is only suitable for a particular gender, ethnicity, or race. Even after organizations master hiring a diverse workforce, retaining the workforce requires an inclusive environment. While we may believe we can measure diversity because it is quantifiable, without an inclusive environment, the crucial connections that attract diverse talent, encourage participation, foster innovation, and lead to business growth will not happen.

Let us say an organization recruits a more significant number of women or People of Color just to check the diversity box, but further steps still need to be taken to create an inclusive environment. If the organization does not provide equal opportunities to develop these employees, the hiring practices are counterproductive to growth and profitability. Ignoring inclusion can lead to higher turnover, less creativity and innovation, and less job satisfaction. Creating an inclusive workplace requires inclusive leadership and organizational culture can only be changed if the senior leadership is on board with the inclusion initiatives. A leader with the vision to create an equitable working environment for all members can provide psychological safety, which leads to greater job satisfaction, higher performance, and more innovation and creativity.

As a result of significant social changes over the past few decades, the concept of workforce DEI is getting a foothold in companies worldwide. Recent studies have shown that companies with diverse executive teams posted larger profit margins than their rivals, compared to companies with relatively little diversity in their upper echelons. Many examples of the potential link between DEI and positive business outcomes exist.

At this point, the research is clear. For example, companies that ranked in the top quartile for ethnic diversity among their executives were 33% more likely to outperform competitors on profits than those in the bottom 25%. Companies with the highest number of women in management were 21% more likely to achieve above-average profitability than those with relatively few women in senior decision-making roles.

Further, companies with at least three women on their boards achieved a higher return on equity and earnings per share over the next five years than those without women. This research suggests better business outcomes through DEI and a link between diverse decision-makers and higher profits.

However, what businesses mean by diversity and inclusion and what they think they must do to achieve it often remains to be discovered. While the awareness and intention might be there, the path toward achieving diversity and inclusion must be clarified. Once again, another dilemma.

INTERSECTIONALITY

Intersectionality is the idea that all forms of oppression are interconnected. To be more specific, the Oxford Dictionary defines intersectionality as "the interconnected nature of social categorizations such as race, class, and gender, regarded as creating overlapping and interdependent systems of discrimination or disadvantage." Recognizing that each person experiences discrimination and oppression uniquely is fundamental to intersectionality. It necessitates consideration of a wide range of factors that can marginalize individuals, including gender, race, class, sexual orientation, physical ability, and more. Coined by Professor Kimberlé Crenshaw in 1989, the term intersectionality was officially included in the Oxford Dictionary in 2015, gaining increasing recognition, especially in the context of women's rights.

Stereotypes, which may be associated with specific genders, races, religions, or countries, often interconnect various elements of identity. Take, for instance, a stereotype concerning Black gay men, which encompasses considerations of race, gender, and sexual orientation. While such a stereotype focuses on a particular subgroup rather than the entire Black community, it remains problematic to imply that all Black gay men share identical traits. The richness of an individual's identity involves numerous factors, making it inappropriate to attribute a rigid set of characteristics to any person.

To further understand this example, the stereotypes about Black gay men that imply that they all gossip, are fashionable, and are always focused on sex, involves considerations of race, gender, and sexual orientation. The complexity of individual identity incorporates numerous factors, making it inappropriate to assign a fixed set of traits to any person.

Without an intersectional lens, our efforts to tackle inequalities and injustice towards women are likely to end up perpetuating systems of inequalities. A Black woman may experience misogyny and racism, but she will experience misogyny differently from a White woman and racism differently from a Black man. Varied stereotypes can exist within broader communities, leading to distinctions such as gender-based stereotypes within a particular racial group. While certain stereotypes may apply broadly to Asian Americans, a closer examination by gender reveals differences in the stereotypes associated with Asian American men and women. For instance, women from a particular racial group may be objectified and considered attractive, while men from the same racial background may face contrasting perceptions.

Even stereotypes attributed to a racial group show inconsistencies when individuals within that group are further categorized by their origin.

JUSTICE

Justice occurs when barriers to resources and career advancement are dismantled. Perceptions of justice can impact important outcomes and should not be ignored. There are various types and levels of justice. For example, distributive justice pertains to employees' perception of fairness in the outcomes they receive from the organization, essentially evaluating whether they receive equitable returns for their contributions.

Procedural justice focuses on employees' perception of fairness in the processes through which outcomes are assigned. Interactional justice relates to employees' perception of the fairness in interpersonal treatment received from authority figures, encompassing aspects like dignity and respect. Research indicates that positive changes in these justice dimensions strongly correlate with job satisfaction and organizational commitment.

Racial justice is distinct from social justice and the broader diversity, equity, and inclusion framework. Social justice encompasses the examination of wealth, privilege, and opportunity distribution within a society, addressing oppression such as ableism, ageism, classism, racism, sexism, and discrimination against the LGBTQIA+ community, individuals from different countries, or those with religious affiliations.

The United States has a lengthy history of unequal and discriminatory treatment based on race, including instances of human chattel enslavement, forced displacement from ancestral homelands, and colonialism. Those who continue to endure the consequences of this harmful treatment are racial and ethnic minorities, especially individuals who identify as Black or African American, Latino, Asian, South Asian or Asian American, Native American or Indigenous,

Middle Eastern or North African, and Native Hawaiian and other Pacific Islanders.

MERITOCRACY

Despite the word's connotation, meritocracy has often become a mighty enemy of equity. When organizations position themselves as meritocracies, they imply that they operate in environments of social equality. Meritocracy may be a value and a goal, but it is not a current reality.

Meritocracy and diversity are conflicting values that cannot be simultaneously achieved. The idea that meritocracy and diversity are incompatible implies that increasing diversity requires compromising on performance or suitability, suggesting that those not in the powerful majority are somehow "lowering the bar." This myth insinuates that the underrepresentation of certain sociodemographic groups is due to inherent differences, reinforcing the notion that certain groups are unsuitable for appointments.

Organizations should avoid using meritocracy as a guise for limited progress on diversity. Instead, organizations have an opportunity to recruit the most qualified individuals, leading to a more accurate representation of the larger population and fostering greater efficiency.

I started my career with the understanding that I would be judged based on merit. That if I did my job and did it well, I would be rewarded and promoted in the same way as everyone else. I soon learned from various experiences that involved exceeding performance expectations and not being promoted that merit was just one part of my ability to succeed within an organization and hold prestige within a community. It was a difficult pill to swallow that I would need to do more than graduate at the top of the class; I would need to possess a mixture of influence, political savvy, and a solid network to achieve the success I was seeking.

MUTING

In 1975, Edwin and Shirley Ardener, a husband-and-wife anthropologist team, coined the term muted group theory (MGT) to describe how language can marginalize people and silence their thoughts, voices, and perspectives. MGT addresses how dominant groups sometimes marginalize sub-dominant groups based on their privileged status in society and is often used to illustrate how power and privileged status impact modes of communication. A fundamental principle of the MGT is that individuals from dominant and sub-dominant groups undergo distinct life experiences shaped by their societal status.

The sub-dominant group's communication style, including a person's accent and vocabulary, is less acceptable than the dominant group's communication style. The sub-dominant group must acquire a communication style consistent with the style preferred by the dominant group to communicate effectively with them. The three tenets of the MGT can mute or silence the expression and thoughts of those who are marginalized. For example, fearing backlash prevents a woman from adopting an authoritative tone. In this way, privilege-dominant groups force the subordinate groups to remain silent.

Though MGT originally addressed gender inequality, we use it to explain the silencing of other marginalized groups, including members of the LGBTQ community, immigrants, People of Color, and people with disabilities. Language becomes intertwined with educational access. Our school systems often only recognize European-based American Standard English, and students who do not adhere to this standard may be placed in remedial classes. As a result, these children do not receive the same access to the resources used by other students.

Many children and parents are forced to give up their culture and language and adapt to the dominant culture, a phenomenon known as subtractive acculturation. Here is something I had to face and consider daily, and this is why African American Vernacular English (AAVE), or Ebonics, is not acceptable for many professional communications. The muted group theory stresses that sub-dominant groups must communicate in a way that is representative of the dominant members. For Black and Brown women, this is detrimental to creativity and efficiency, creating disadvantages for organizations that seek to thrive in a highly competitive environment. The non-dominant group is constantly scrutinized and judged in corporate and business settings.

Let us take the case of Shakira, who often feels muted and silenced at work. During meetings, when Shakira speaks, she is non-dominant and is frequently corrected by the dominant players in the room. For example, when they finish her sentences, when they "translate" something she has already said, or when they claim that she did not speak loud enough, demonstrating the need for their interpretation. This stark example is evidence of the perpetuation of workplace repression for many minority women.

PRIVILEGE

Privilege is also a very polarizing word. Even the word polarizing can bring about polarization. The term privilege implies the ability to benefit. White privilege is not the assumption that everything a white person has accomplished is unearned. Many White people who have reached a high level of success have worked extremely hard to achieve high levels in their fields. Instead, White privilege should be perceived as an inherent advantage, independent of one's income or exerted effort. These advantages represent what could be termed "the power of normalcy." If public spaces and amenities appear tailored to one racial group, relegating the needs of people from other races to designated sections, it signifies an underlying issue. White individuals are more inclined to navigate the world with the expectation that their needs will be readily accommodated, while People of Color move through the world aware that their needs are often marginalized. Recognizing this involves acknowledging existing disparities.

White individuals are also more likely to encounter positive depictions of people resembling them in the news, television shows, and movies. They are more likely to be treated as unique individuals rather than representatives of a stereotyped racial identity. In essence, they are more frequently humanized and given the benefit of the doubt, receiving compassion, being recognized for individual potential, and overcoming mistakes. White privilege, represented by the "power of normalcy" and the "power of the benefit of the doubt," are not merely subconscious remnants of historical discrimination; instead, they are intentional outcomes of racism, facilitating the continual recreation of inequality. These powers would not persist without the prior existence of systemic racism. Systemic racism cannot endure unless these powers maintain influence.

Inclusion incorporates the tenets of cultural competence—the ability to discern, respect, and consider cultural differences in decision-making, problem-solving, and conflict resolution. Ignorance around White privilege persists as research studies continue to find significant differences regarding race relations between European Americans and

African Americans, with White Americans often making light of racist acts against minorities that are often tied to White privilege. A double standard usually occurs when White people feel their racial identity is threatened; they often respond with various acts of racism against those in the out-group in an attempt to protect members of the in-group. This double standard has persisted for many years, as most Whites continue to be ignorant about race disparities and the invisible advantages among their group. For example, though White Americans consistently excel higher than racial minorities overall, from a wealth and social status perspective, Whites generally do not associate their success with being privileged.

Researchers describe this phenomenon as the things members of dominant groups are taught not to know. Scholars refer to this phenomenon as epistemic ignorance – a concept that encapsulates the knowledge gaps deliberately instilled within members of dominant groups. There are many things they are encouraged not to see and are rewarded for doing so. Therefore, not knowing the dominant group muddles the consequences of an unjust system, so they do not have to consider their role in perpetuating the injustices placed on those in the out-group and, simultaneously, see themselves as "good." White people are not the only people capable of perpetuating White supremacy. The system is set up to have others replicate that behavior.

RACISM

According to the Britannica Encyclopedia, racism is the belief that certain human groups have inherent behavioral traits, leading to the justification of dividing them based on the perceived superiority of one race over another. Racism can also encompass prejudice, discrimination, or hostility directed at individuals due to race or ethnicity. Contemporary forms of racism often stem from societal perceptions of biological distinctions between people. These perspectives may manifest as social behaviors, practices, beliefs, or political systems that categorize different races as inherently superior or inferior, attributing presumed inheritable traits, abilities, or qualities. There have been efforts to validate racist beliefs through scientific means, but such attempts have been overwhelmingly discredited. If genuine change is to occur, it is crucial to become familiar with the following concepts surrounding racism.

Embedded in our cultural definitions of expectations, correctness, professionalism, intelligence, beauty, and value is systemic racism. Racism includes the policies and practices entrenched in established institutions (education, healthcare, housing, employment, wealth, representation in leadership positions) that exclude or promote designated groups.

Antiracism is an active and conscious effort to work against multidimensional aspects of racism. Racism scholar, Ibram X. Kendi, says one is either racist or anti-racist. There is no room for neutrality, and there is no such thing as a non-racist. Personal accountability and action are at the heart of being an anti-racist.

White Fragility is the propensity of white people to fend off suggestions of racism. This can manifest through absurd denials such as "I do not see color," or overly emotional displays of defensiveness or solidarity.

Although scientists have clearly misinterpreted data to fit racist views, the legitimacy of facts and research, science, and data may be the only place we can go. In my research involving critical race theory (CRT), social identity theory (SIT), and social constructionism theory (SCT), participants were asked to describe their lived experiences of diversity and recruiting for diversity. Using a framework of CRT, which allowed me to purport that racism is real, I was then able to explore how our identities and need to belong impact race, inclusion, and equity. Using a scholarly approach and theories to observe phenomena allowed for life-changing dialogue and potential solutions based on the research.

SHRM's report, *The Journey to Equity and Inclusion*, found a need for more awareness about racial inequality in the workplace. According to a SHRM survey, 47% of Black HR professionals surveyed said they do not feel safe voicing their opinions about racial justice issues in the workplace, while only 28% of White HR professionals said the same. However, Black and White workers generally agreed that discussions about race can be uncomfortable. By engaging in thoughtful discussions about race, you can play a role in guiding workplaces and communities toward a new era characterized by respect, understanding, honesty, and inclusion. Let the emphasis be on genuine dialogue rather than performative or symbolic gestures.

STEREOTYPES

A stereotype is a widely held but fixed and oversimplified image or idea of a particular type of person or thing. Although all stereotypes involve generalizations, not all generalizations qualify as stereotypes. Stereotypes are widely shared oversimplifications of a specific group, while generalizations may stem more from personal experiences rather than being universally accepted. In the United States, certain racial groups have been associated with stereotypes, such as excelling in math, athletics, or dancing. Asians are stereotyped as good at math or bad drivers. Jewish people are stereotyped as being good with money and shrewd.

These stereotypes are so pervasive that most Americans could readily identify the racial group known for prowess in basketball. When one engages in stereotyping, one perpetuates cultural myths already present in a specific society.

THE LENS OF WHITENESS

A culprit of White privilege is the role of *whitewashing*. Whitewashing is a process that denies race and, at the same time, promotes White culture. In the workplace, whitewashing is responsible for maintaining White culture as the dominant culture of business politics. The workplace involves meaningful relationships and power politics that have a significant effect on the experiences of employees. Through hiring, firing, and promotion, the role whitewashing plays in the workplace can be powerful. Day-to-day practices attempt to reject racial politics in the workplace while simultaneously superimposing white culture.

White privilege is also discussed in terms of White complicity. Similarly, White complicity involves unconscious negative beliefs and attitudes toward minorities and the idea that White people benefit from those group privileges of racism that, at the same time, marginalize People of Color. Some posit that all Whites are complicit because they can benefit from White privilege, even though these privileges have not been asked for and cannot be renounced. The starting point for addressing these issues and creating a shared language with People of Color, however, is for Whites to acknowledge complicity rather than deny it.

The *white complicity* philosophy argues that if White Americans engage in discussions about their privileges rather than resist these discussions, there is a greater possibility that alliances can be established between the privileged and the non-privileged. These alliances can ultimately resolve the unjust system that continues to exist in American society.

This occurs despite the constant inundation of information regarding institutional racism in our daily lives. News detailing the deaths of unarmed Black, Native American/Indigenous, and Muslim individuals at the hands of the police and armed White civilians is ubiquitous. Statistics highlighting the alarming rates of incarceration and racial disparities among the incarcerated are hard to overlook. Films like *I'm Not Your Negro, 13th, Selma, Moonlight, Fruitvale Station*, and *12 Years a Slave* (to mention a few) surround us. Frederick Douglass and W. E. B. Du Bois, James Baldwin, Toni Morrison, and Ta-Nehisi Coates have written about the struggles for the past two centuries. The Black Lives Matter movement is tirelessly advocating for others to join their campaign against systemic racism and its violent impacts.

The personalities and policies that emerged in the 2016 presidential election have made issues of White dominance evident and repugnant to White individuals. Previously, they had managed to suppress awareness of the cries of the oppressed. Although more people appear to desire change, I still encounter bewilderment, shame, guilt, and a reluctance to address the issue of White privilege from many. This privilege itself grants us the ability to disregard the constant physical and emotional pain that others are compelled to endure.

WHITE SUPREMACY

In 1946, one of the most brilliant minds, Albert Einstein, wrote:

> There is, however, a somber point in the social outlook of Americans. Their sense of equality and human dignity is

mainly limited to men of white skin. Even among these [men of white skin], there are prejudices of which I as a Jew am clearly conscious; but they are not important in comparison with the attitude of the Whites towards their fellow citizens of darker complexion, particularly towards Negroes. The more I feel like an American, the more this situation pains me. I can escape the feeling of complicity in it only by speaking out.

White supremacy envisions a society where White people are elevated as the ideal for humanity, while everyone else is perceived as a deficient version, with Black people specifically cast as the most flawed. White supremacy is a belief system and ideology that asserts the inherent superiority of White people over people of other racial or ethnic backgrounds. It promotes the notion that White individuals and the White culture should dominate and control societies, institutions, and resources. White supremacists often advocate for the preservation of racial purity, the enforcement of discriminatory laws and policies, and the exclusion or subjugation of non-White individuals.

White supremacy has a long history rooted in colonialism, imperialism, and the Transatlantic Slave Trade. It has manifested in various forms, including slavery, segregation, systemic racism, and hate crimes. White supremacists may express their ideology through organized groups, such as White supremacist organizations, neo-Nazi movements, or the Ku Klux Klan, as well as through online platforms and individual acts of violence. It is important to note that White supremacy is widely condemned as an oppressive and unjust ideology by most societies and organizations around the world. The principles of equality, diversity, and respect for all individuals, regardless of their race, ethnicity, or background, are central to promoting a just and inclusive society.

White individuals generally see themselves as positively represented and normalized in media, while people of other races are often stereotyped, marginalized, or underrepresented.

It is important to note that acknowledging White privilege does not diminish personal struggles or deny that White individuals can face hardships. Instead, it recognizes that systemic advantages exist and aims to promote understanding, empathy, and efforts to address and dismantle these structural inequalities. That said, White privilege is still a privilege.

WHITE NARRATIVE

The term *white narrative* typically refers to the dominant societal perspective or storylines that are shaped and perpetuated by White people or White culture. It encompasses the historical, cultural, and social narratives that have been constructed from a predominantly White perspective and often center on the experiences, values, and interests of White individuals or groups. In many societies, White narratives have historically held privileged positions and have been ingrained in various institutions, including education, media, and politics. These narratives often overlook or marginalize the experiences, perspectives, and contributions of non-White individuals and communities. They can reinforce stereotypes, perpetuate systemic inequalities, and uphold structures of power that benefit White individuals or groups. The concept of challenging or deconstructing White narratives has emerged as part of broader movements for social justice and equity. It involves recognizing and questioning the biases and assumptions embedded in these narratives, amplifying marginalized voices and experiences, and striving for a more inclusive and diverse range of perspectives in shaping societal narratives.

White default is best understood within the framework of the socially constructed concept of *whiteness*, recognized as the standard and central racial identity. Whiteness, being the benchmark against which racial minorities are measured, is thus considered the default standard.

The establishment of whiteness as the default creates a reality in which White individuals, because of their racial identity, do not face the challenges experienced by those with minority identification. Whiteness as the default confers socioeconomic privileges and advantages over racial minorities, which may go unnoticed by White individuals not subjected to an alternative standard of adversity.

We see White default in action when products, media, or cultural representations primarily feature or center around White individuals, perspectives, or experiences, implicitly assuming a White audience as the norm. This can be observed in various contexts, such as advertising, literature, film, and educational materials, where non-White individuals are often underrepresented or portrayed in stereotypical roles.

The most recent adaptation of the movie, *The Little Mermaid*, pushed the envelope against White default. The story, based on Hans Christian Andersen's fairy tale, is set in an underwater world. Despite the fantastical setting, the characters are predominantly depicted with Eurocentric features and features that align with Western norms.

In the recent adaptation, the red-haired, fair-skinned protagonist, Ariel, is played by the brown-skinned, naturally locked, hair Halle Bailey and no longer conforms to the traditional Western standard of beauty. Additionally, the supporting characters and the overall cultural context of the film reflect a diverse instead of a Eurocentric perspective.

The concept of White default is evident when the default assumption in casting, character design, and cultural representation tends to align with a White or Western norm, unintentionally sidelining or marginalizing other racial and cultural perspectives.

DEVELOPING AGENTS OF INCLUSION AND BELONGING

To truly reach inclusion and belonging, we must turn away from the narrative to which we should assimilate. Instead, individuals need to embrace their individuality. Going through an age of enlightenment, the world is recognizing the need for equity in the workspace and the current lack of equity. People of Color have been impacted. It is all interrelated. The real question is, how do we deal with the next 22 years during the pending demographic shift?

During the recent *Diversity, Equity, Inclusion & Accessibility: Trends, Updates and the DEIA Leadership Forum*, DEI advocates and business leaders discussed the importance of belonging as it relates to inclusion and belonging efforts. The panelists emphasized that to have innovative solutions in business systems, it is time to embrace new thinking. However, creating an inclusive situation that allows for individualism can be challenging for organizations that default to operating through command and control. Intentional inclusion leads to improved belonging. Permeance and sustainability will occur when inclusion is baked into our policies and practices.

The objectives of DEI initiatives must go beyond meeting compliance goals to effectively drive a sense of belonging and positively impact the business. To build a culture that supports belonging, companies need to align DEI to their values and decision-making processes. Businesses can increase that sense of belonging for their employees by manifesting behaviors and by participating in the following actions that foster inclusion; Behaviors such as listening while practicing emotional intelligence (EI) and cultural intelligence (CQ). Both EI and CQ involve active listening and being cognizant of bias. To deepen listening skills, it is vital to acknowledge the feelings of others and commit to remaining educated on cultural concepts.

ERGs and DEI councils create platforms that ensure psychological safety and pro mote the feeling of inclusion. During these sessions, ensure that there are opportunities for storytelling that allow employees to feel seen and heard.

Business leaders should embrace a broader vision of success that encompasses learning, innovation, flexibility, equity, and human dignity. In addition, benchmarking results through employee surveys allows the business to measure success or determine areas of improvement. Leaders are encouraged to make inclusion and belonging a priority. This can be done when employees are celebrated for their uniqueness, rewarded, and recognized for their contributions to the work environment. For me, this could have boosted my self-confidence early in my career.

Creating a sense of belonging pays emotional and financial dividends. When belonging is fostered from within, it permeates to a business's client base, which can lead to increased revenue. For example, when employees understand how to effectively use culturally specific language, they can use that same language to drive customer loyalty. Understanding that everyone has strengths and weaknesses, organizations will create an environment where everyone belongs. As businesses perfect behaviors needed to achieve organizational cultures rich in purpose and strong in mutual respect, those cultures will foster environments in which individuals and teams build and maintain strong relationships. This, in turn, allows employees to bring their best selves to work.

Organizations are beginning to increasingly recognize the urgency of advancing equity initiatives. Although companies raced to make racial justice commitments in the summer of 2020, only some have made meaningful progress. Some have hired DEI staff to solve these magnanimous issues. Some organizations have made minimal investments in their programming. No one would disagree that the workforce of the future will be more diverse than ever. Generational differences, such as Gen Z and Millennials, heavily prioritize company values. Companies are scrambling to make more effective and measurable changes. The changes are not only complex but often feel impossible. This can be seen in the need for more progress. Research shows that while many companies are making commitments, they often need to collect data on these issues, strategically invest in programming that actually moves the needle, or hold their leaders accountable for change.

In my dissertation, *The Impact of Executive Hiring Decisions within Homeless Services Providers,* a profound inquiry unfolded – an inquiry that touched upon the inter play of power dynamics, biases, and their influence on the provision of services. My study aimed to dissect the phenomenon where those in positions of power often dictate the hiring decisions within organizations that support minority communities. In my research, a critical nexus was unearthed, that connected human resources, public policy, and equity, as the investigation delved into the inequities embedded within staffing practices that directly impact the quality of social services provided to the homeless. There were complex realities to unpack. Take, for instance, the challenges faced by homeless services, exacerbated by systemic racism. The endeavor to hire a diverse array of employees to better address the needs of minority clients, while well-intentioned, can introduce intricate challenges.

My study raised questions about how various hiring practices within social service programs can genuinely impact the outcomes for the marginalized communities they serve. The goal of my study was to bridge this knowledge gap and scrutinize the hiring practices of senior employees who wield decision-making authority. A notable void emerged; a lack of awareness surrounding formal processes to ensure diverse hiring within their respective organizations. The findings underscored the critical need for not only diverse hiring but also for the integration of cultural competence. The participants' sentiments emphasized the dire necessity for individuals with the capacity to understand, respect, and navigate diverse cultural backgrounds; an ability that enhances the delivery of services that cater to an array of communities.

The crux of my study's findings unveiled a realm where the journey from cultural incompetence to cultural competence can dismantle barriers, elevate services, and bring about real change. The ramifications of cultural incompetence are profound, perpetuating biases, reinforcing inequalities, and hindering the efficacy of services. My study underscored the imperative for decision-makers to heed the call for diverse hiring practices intertwined with cultural competence.

The goal of my research was to find ways to identify and dismantle the facade of cultural incompetence while underscoring the profound implications it has on equity, inclusion, and social services. The journey from our current landscape to one defined by cultural competence is not merely an academic endeavor; it is a transformative odyssey that promises to reshape organizations and societies alike. We must continue to pull back the layers word by word, phrase by phrase, and action by action to see a true transformation.

II
TRAUMA AND DRAMA

"I have no love for America…"
- Frederick Douglass

Frederick Douglass' powerful quote was no doubt iterated from a place of trauma and based on the fact that America had no love for Frederick Douglass and his people. The system was set up to make Black people believe that nature had made us inferior, particularly to White people. Douglass challenged that system. Douglass' relationship with America was extremely complicated.

Douglass' sentiments toward America resonate with the emotionally charged love-hate relationship I have with a country that my ancestors played a significant role in building—a country I love, but one that does not always reciprocate that love. I sense that Douglass embodies this complex dilemma.

To question why someone should respect differences is challenging to anyone of any race, walk, or creed. Everyone wants to be respected. I often think of Rev. Dr. Martin Luther King, Jr. and the level of emotional intelligence he displayed when asked to represent and speak for all "the Negroes in America." Dr. King always knew that we were not a monolith at the time, although the rest of the country was not. Somehow, he managed to hold his course and focused, sometimes painfully, while conveying his message for Civil Rights. When I watch recordings of his speech, I can feel the trauma as a result of the drama he was dealing with during the civil rights movement.

The trauma and drama are real. According to the Association for Behavioral and Cognitive Therapies, research indicates at least 63% of Black Americans, along with 47% of Latin Americans, 6% of Asian Americans, 5% of Native/Indigenous Americans, and 4% of multiracial individuals endorse experiencing at least one racially charged trauma in their life. In fact, race-based traumatic stress is associated with a number of individual harms, including depression, anxiety, headaches, upset stomach, humiliation, difficulty sleeping, and nightmares.

The portrayal of unarmed Black and Brown individuals being killed by police in the media has a profound impact on the mental health of many minorities. This shared experience has led many of us to experience Post-Traumatic Stress Disorder (PTSD). The repeated exposure to such traumatic events, often sensationalized and disseminated through various media channels, can lead to heightened stress, anxiety, and a sense of helplessness among individuals from marginalized communities. I can attest to this phenomenon.

The constant barrage of graphic images and narratives depicting police violence not only perpetuates a cycle of fear but also reinforces a disturbing reality for many minorities.

Witnessing people who look like themselves being subjected to violence and injustice can create a deep sense of vulnerability and distress.

Furthermore, the lack of accountability and justice in many high-profile cases intensifies the trauma, fostering a pervasive mistrust in the system. The cumulative effect of these experiences can manifest as PTSD symptoms, including flashbacks, nightmares, and hypervigilance, impacting the mental well-being of individuals who already face systemic challenges and discrimination.

Addressing the mental health consequences of media portrayals of police violence is crucial. It underscores the importance of advocating for more responsible media coverage, increased awareness of the psychological impact on marginalized communities, and the necessity of comprehensive support systems for those affected by the trauma associated with these portrayals.

This book has been challenging to write because each month, DEI has been under attack and attitudes fluctuate. For the last few years, it seems that the anti-DEI sentiment has gained traction. In a time where the post-George Floyd era was actually shifting the public's consciousness, old habits have indeed been hard to break. The Supreme Court's decision to end Affirmative Action and strip away LGBTQIA+ rights has been the cherry on top of the DEI hate train. The critiques of DEI have been escalating; in 2020, the 45th President of the United States issued a diversity training ban, and almost three years later, conservatives are hoping to limit corporate DEI efforts.

The chief diversity officer for the state of Virginia recently stated that "DEI is dead." Martin D. Brown, who has been serving as chief diversity, opportunity, and inclusion officer for Governor Glenn Youngkin since November 2022, made this bold statement in a speech at Virginia Military

Institution. In a statement to *The Washington Post*, Brown asserted, "It's proven that institutions achieve more with a more diverse and inclusive workforce...however, equity has become a tradeoff for excellence."

This notion becomes apparent in certain situations where the drive for equity appears to clash with or compromise the pursuit of excellence. Personally, I have encountered instances where managers bluntly expressed reluctance to consider a diversity hire, citing concerns about compromising candidate quality. It is bewildering to me that they feel at ease sharing such sentiments directly with me, implying that I am somehow considered inferior.

Detractors often argue that hiring for diversity may prioritize diversity over perceived merit, suggesting that the pursuit of equity could lower standards or compromise outcomes. Curiously, these concerns seem absent when individuals are selected based on nepotism or cronyism, where qualifications take a back seat to personal connections. In such cases, the focus shifts to who you know or who knows you, raising questions about the consistency of these objections.

What is the future of DEI? When this question was asked to an audience on LinkedIn via a poll, the results garnered some interesting findings. Out of over 500 responses, 40% of respondents felt that the future of DEI needs to be more investment and funding in DEI. In addition, 25% of respondents indicated that there will be less focus on race and racism in DEI efforts. Whereas 19% of respondents said that what we are seeing now is the end of DEI as we know it, and 16% felt that DEI would stay the same. Several factors point to a shift in the DEI landscape.

DEI in higher education is facing repeated attacks. Florida Governor Ron DeSantis has become one of the most vocal figures in the anti-DEI movement. In May of

2023, DeSantis signed legislation prohibiting public colleges and universities from funding DEI initiatives in the state of Florida. An anti-DEI legislation tracker from Bestcolleges.com revealed that as of June 2023, there were several states where anti-DEI legislation had been introduced or approved, including Texas, North Carolina, South Carolina, Georgia, Alabama, Louisiana, and Oklahoma.

According to a 2023 NBC News article, DEI roles are shrinking. *The Seattle Times* reported in January 2023 that tech layoffs are hitting DEI roles, which are seeing sharp declines. Hady Mendez is a DEI practitioner who worked for a large tech company until she was laid off in March 2023. Mendez, who is the founder and CEO of Boldly Speaking LLC, shared that while she thinks corporations are sold on the "business case" for DEI, she anticipates pushback. "I think [some] organizations might use the current environment as an excuse to be compliant...but to otherwise move away from prioritizing DEI initiatives that were never a priority in the first place."

The results of a subsequent LinkedIn poll indicated that many feel that DEI will become less focused on race. "From 2020 to early 2022, I believe companies focused a lot on racial equity and wanted to do their part to level the playing field," shared DEI practitioner Lambert Odeh Jr. "Unfortunately, starting in mid-2022, I started to see equality being the focus again." Odeh expressed concerns that progress will be halted with a move away from an equity focus. Odeh further purported, "We've learned a lot about equity versus equality in the last couple of years, so we unfortunately know this is all headed back towards the status quo."

I have been part of conversations where people express exhaustion around the topic of DEI, and I strongly believe that we cannot afford to lose focus on the importance of equity. However, it is time to approach this work differently.

I often tell fellow DEI professionals who feel weary that it is not our sole responsibility to fix DEI issues. Instead, we should be receiving committed and unwavering support and direction from the highest levels of the organization or agency, empowering us to implement the necessary changes. I distinctly remember when I started my DEI journey, the CEO promised to be the driving force, ready to remove any obstacles related to equity that I might encounter. In less than a year, I discovered that I couldn't even obtain a butter knife, let alone the 'machete that would cut down obstacles' that the CEO had promised. Unfortunately, I consistently observed this pattern around DEI over time.

Anti-racism should be the nucleus of any DEI efforts; a failure to prioritize racial equity in DEI work means that inequities will continue to persist. The result of the divestment from DEI will have deleterious effects on racial diversity in the workplace. Deprioritizing DEI means that racial disparities will widen. Many of those hit hardest by layoffs, particularly in tech, are Black and Brown workers. Workplaces that adopt race-neutral policies have an opportunity to hinder their ability to find the best and most competitive talent.

Historically, DEI initiatives have always been first on the chopping block when resources get tight for organizations, especially in today's volatile economy. Despite the evident need to persist in prioritizing DEI, it is highly probable that the future will bring about more cutbacks and diminished funding for DEI initiatives.

Although anti-DEI sentiments are rising, the good news is that DEI is far from over. We are experiencing just another of the many metamorphoses that naturally occur in workplaces and within all environments. Our DEI GPS systems are just recalculating. The reality is that DEI cannot die as long as there are people. Our diversity is what makes us, and if we want to coexist peacefully in these shared spaces,

DEI is a requirement. Folks may want to call it something else, but the core goal—fostering understanding and fairness amongst people—continues to be the same.

I have been to numerous conferences, and an interesting phenomenon has been observed. Black women are hurting. Yes, Black women are still hurting, and having dozens of tear-filled conversations with complete strangers and lots of colleagues has ended in the same conclusion; women and Black women are struggling to feel safe in the workplace.

Let me share how my traumatic stress shows up. While writing this book, I had a horrible dream in which I took a wrong turn and walked through an active construction site. One of the construction workers saw me and immediately reached for a weapon. He picked up a bat, then a crowbar, and then eventually a nail gun and had it pointed at my head in fear. He did not understand English. I was trying to communicate with him and tell him that I was looking for the exit out of the construction site. I yelled, "I am not a crack patient!" There were children outside the door as he backed out slowly toward the door, he was leading me to. I tried to motion with my eyes and body that he should lower the nail gun, afraid that it would go off. But he did not want to drop it until he saw the look of fear in the children's eyes. He was absolutely terrified of me.

In the same dream, as soon as I stepped out the door, the police handed me a vial that was filled with murky orange and red material. I asked why they gave me this, and they replied, "I thought you would want to know what your son did." At that, I looked to the street, and a young Black man was sitting on the ground with their hands handcuffed behind their back. The alleged perpetrators had a stunned look in their eyes. A young Black girl looked at me and said,

"Your son ran over a girl." I replied, "Not my son." I looked at my son and cried. I went toward my son, who had so much defeat and sadness in his eyes, and I cried and wept uncontrollably until I woke myself up out of this nightmare.

I was able to remind myself when I woke up that it was just a dream. I reminded myself that I am a good citizen; I am not a thief or a crackhead. In real life, my son is a good person, and he is not on drugs; he is responsible, he is not a murderer. This is the trauma we keep in our Black bodies.

Images and treatment from society cause many of us to have night terrors. I often have multiple night terrors. Sadly (if sadly is strong enough a word), these terrors manifest in real life as mistaken identity, false accusation, and being blamed, sentenced, and punished further for crimes we have not committed. These occurrences are everyday experiences for Black people and minorities in America. Then, we are expected to go to work and show up and be our absolute best amidst microaggressions, false accusations, blaming and condescending tones, glances, and a daily effort to prove to our employees that we are safe, that we are trustworthy, that we are good people.

In a particular organization, earnest efforts were made to enhance diversity and inclusion across its workforce. These initiatives were driven by good intentions and aimed at creating a more equitable and representative environment. However, one particular incident highlighted the potential unintended consequences of such efforts. A Black woman, whom I will call Mieesha, who had been an employee at the company for several years, found herself deeply traumatized by the diversity initiatives. While Mieesha appreciated the intention behind the efforts, the implementation inadvertently led to a situation where her identity was spotlighted in uncomfortable ways. She began to feel like she was only valued for her racial background rather than her skills, experiences, and accomplishments.

In an attempt to promote open dialogue about racial experiences, the company organized a series of workshops where employees were encouraged to share their stories. During one of these sessions, Mieesha found herself overwhelmed by emotions as she recounted instances of racial discrimination she had faced throughout her life. The experience of sharing her painful memories in a public setting was deeply distressing, and she felt exposed and vulnerable. Moreover, the constant focus on diversity made her feel like she was being singled out. She wanted to be recognized for her professional achievements and contributions rather than solely for her racial identity. As a result, she started to withdraw from team activities and interactions, fearing that her every action was being observed through a racial lens.

While the organization intended to foster inclusivity, the unintended consequences of this well-meaning effort had a profound impact on Mieesha's mental and emotional well-being. It underscored the importance of not only implementing diversity initiatives but also ensuring that they are carried out sensitively and with a keen understanding of the potential impact they might have on individual experiences. This incident serves as a reminder that the complexity of human experiences requires a nuanced and empathetic approach to ensure the well-being of all employees, regardless of their background.

A well-known tech company has repeatedly been in the news for reports from its workers, specifically women and minorities, who are receiving unfair treatment. In addition, I was personally made aware of the organization's lack of honoring accommodations for people with diverse abilities. In fact, friends and family members I know who have worked for the company describe unfair working conditions for women and minorities. Not honoring daycare needs, not providing proper safety equipment, not providing adequate management direction and supervision, not protecting employees' rights…and so on.

Individuals from diverse backgrounds, including women, minorities, and those facing economic challenges, are eager to advance within an organization that fosters trust. Latinos share narratives about being trained for new opportunities within this company but never received the promotion or the chance. Recent investigations found that some of this company's warehouses have injury rates as high as triple the industry average. There have been several criticisms and concerns raised regarding this company's impact on Black people. It is important to note that these issues are not unique to this company and can be found within the broader context of systemic inequalities and challenges faced by marginalized communities.

A well-known e-commerce and distribution company has faced criticism for its treatment of workers, including allegations of unfair labor practices, inadequate pay, and poor working conditions. These concerns are not specific to Black employees but affect a diverse range of workers. However, given the demographics of its workforce, which includes a significant number of Black employees, these issues can disproportionately impact them. There have been claims of racial discrimination and bias in the company's hiring, promotion, and termination practices. In 2020, a group of workers from this organization filed a lawsuit alleging racial discrimination, unequal pay, and inadequate opportunities for advancement.

While the lawsuit is ongoing, it highlights concerns about potential disparities faced by Black employees. The organization has faced criticism for algorithmic systems that exhibit bias, including in hiring and product recommendation processes. These algorithms can inadvertently perpetuate existing racial biases and result in discriminatory outcomes. For example, there have been instances where the company's facial recognition technology showed a higher error rate when identifying individuals with darker skin tones, leading to concerns about racial bias.

The company's expansion and dominance in the retail sector have had mixed effects on local communities, including Black communities. The company's growth has been associated with the closure of local businesses, leading to job losses and economic disruption. This can disproportionately affect communities already facing socio-economic challenges, including Black communities. It is important to note that while these concerns have been raised, they may not apply universally to all of its employees or customers. It is essential to evaluate each issue on its own merits and consider the broader systemic context in which they arise.

CHURCH

You are probably wondering why we are discussing church. Well, it is simple, the church is not exempt from DEI initiatives. Marginalized people are finding that the church, the place they worship, is inflicting the same trauma they experience in the workforce.

It is not a secret that the most segregated place and time in America is on Sunday during most church services. Recently, the church I attended experienced a level of racial tension due to an attempt to "build the bridge." The phrase originated during the civil rights movement of the 1950s and 1960s, when African Americans and other minority groups faced systemic racial discrimination and segregation across various aspects of society, including places of worship. Despite the message of equality and inclusion preached by many religious faiths, churches themselves were often divided along racial lines. African Americans had their churches, often referred to as "Black churches," while White congregations maintained their separate churches.

In post-Civil Rights, many churches integrated. With the integration of different racial/ethnic backgrounds, there has been an influx in racial tensions. In my situation, my church asked me to consult with them on DEI initiatives. However, after meeting with me, they decided to bring someone else to head the DEI initiative. Unfortunately, "building the bridge" was met with many congregants leaving the church. In fact, it prompted my family and me to reconsider our place of worship. This is just another example of how DEI has intertwined with another aspect of my life. It also highlights how many are not ready to effectively implement DEI initiatives.

The phrase "the most segregated places in America" serves as a reminder of the historical and contemporary challenges surrounding racial integration within religious institutions. The state of the church around racism, segregation, and the resulting trauma is one of the most powerful examples of the dilemma that is diversity. It is important to note that this statement does not apply to all churches or religious communities in America, as there are many diverse and inclusive congregations actively working to promote racial unity and understanding.

PLAGUES IN THE ENVIRONMENT

Macroaggressions encompass societal-level events or policies that are racist, such as the overrepresentation of African Americans in the criminal justice system, police brutality, and the murders of African Americans, as exemplified in the cases of George Floyd or Breonna Taylor. These cases represent instances of meso-level aggressions that manifest as race-based traumas within specific communities.

Microaggressions encompass instances of direct individual interactions and encounters with racism, sexism, heterosexism, and nationalism. Examples may range from individuals clutching their purses when passing young African American men to questioning someone of diverse racial background about their origins. It is important to note that microaggressions can be unintentional yet still carry a significant adverse impact. The repercussions of race-based traumatic stress parallel those of other forms of trauma and adversity, and the toll from these experiences accumulates over time.

For instance, microaggressions related to my race have manifested in subtle, everyday actions or comments conveying demeaning or negative attitudes toward Black women with unique names. I am named after my mother, Theola, who was inspired (by an Angel, to be exact) to name her daughter Thelá once she had one. Despite this beautiful gesture, it has been a source of discomfort for as long as I can recall. I have often contemplated using my middle name, Rachelle, to avoid encounters where mostly White individuals attempt to dictate how my name should be spelled and pronounced.

On several occasions, people have insinuated that my mother did not know how to spell or properly place the accent since my name was supposed to be French. I vividly remember a humiliating incident during one of my first executive meetings where I was the only Black person present. Two White women engaged in a debate about the origin of my name as if I were not in the room. One claimed my name was from Newark, NJ, while the other spoke for me, defending my name as if I were absent. This microaggression occurred almost 20 years ago, and I am still in the process of recovering. This brings us to the next issue: post-traumatic stress disorder (PTSD).

PTSD & RBTS: Unveiling the Trauma

Post-traumatic stress disorder (PTSD) and vicarious race-based traumatic stress (RBTS) stand as prevailing consequences of aggression. For BIPOCs (Black, Indigenous, People of Color), the risk of facing traumatic events that mimic PTSD symptoms is notably elevated. The awareness of racism and discrimination further compounds this, leading to RBTS with its myriad adversities such as depression, anxiety, headaches, gastrointestinal issues, humiliation, sleep disturbances, nightmares, loss of appetite, hypervigilance, crying spells, difficulty concentrating, low self-esteem, and avoidance behaviors.

The research underscores the pervasive racial trauma experienced by BIPOCs, with 63% of Black Americans, 47% of Latin Americans, 6% of Asian Americans, 5% of American Indians or Alaskan Natives, and 4% of multiracial individuals acknowledging at least one racially charged trauma in their lifetime. This trauma extends beyond initial hiring, often resulting in belittlement, neglect, or dismissal.

Reflecting on my role as a DEI coach during the Forum on Workplace Inclusion conference, I encountered the stark reality of DEI leaders grappling with trauma. In a single day, counseling approximately ten individuals, the majority being Black, Latino, and Asian women in DEI leadership roles, I witnessed the profound impact of their struggles. Tears were shed, and it became evident that DEI leaders were hurting and traumatized, feeling bamboozled, scared, anxious, depressed, and like failures. This resonated with my own experiences, fostering a deeper connection.

Driving Diversity, Achieving Equity: Navigating the Challenges

A diverse workforce and leadership bring unique perspectives and life experiences, contributing to innovation and success. Suppressing these perspectives hampers the effective advancement of diversity. To drive diversity forward, we need professional courage that transcends our hurts and trauma.

Equity demands proactive efforts. Pay inequity, for instance, is not rooted in women's failure to negotiate but in discriminatory systems and practices. The solution lies in recognizing and rectifying inequities, creating environments where asking for more is not daunting but encouraged as the norm.

Inclusion requires leaders to commit mindfully, to fostering workplace cultures that embrace diverse talents. This requires purposeful action, not relying on magical occurrences. Leaders who prioritize inclusion and surround themselves with diverse voices set the tone for an inclusive culture. They create spaces where varied perspectives are not just presented but respectfully explored, contributing to an environment where every individual feels physically, psychologically, emotionally, and socially safe to contribute their unique skills and gifts.

Leaders who purposefully and meaningfully surround themselves with diverse employees make it safe for them to present various perspectives that are respectfully explored.

III
FACT OR FICTION

"When people get used to preferential treatment, equal treatment seems like discrimination."

– Thomas Sowell

Faulty narratives occur when they are conveyed by those who have not experienced the story. Take critical race theory (CRT) for example. CRT has been the subject of debate, and heated debates have occurred regarding K-12 educators teaching CRT in classrooms. There is ongoing debate about whether CRT serves as a tool for understanding how American racism has influenced public policy or if it fosters divisive discussions pitting People of Color against White individuals.

Kevin Brown, a longtime professor at Indiana University Maurer School of Law, was one of the participants of the original CRT workshop held in 1989 in Madison,

Wisconsin. Kevin Brown maintained that CRT is a framework that helps us understand how race and racism continue to shape the meaning of racial inequality in our dominant culture, our concepts of equality laws, and our institutional governmental and private practices.

Originating in legal analysis frameworks in the late 1970s and early 1980s, key tenets of CRT were developed by legal scholars such as Derrick Bell, Kimberlé Crenshaw, and Richard Delgado. An example illustrating CRT's core idea is the 1930s practice of government officials delineating areas as poor financial risks based on racial composition, leading banks to deny mortgages to Black residents. Modern-day discriminatory patterns persist through seemingly race-neutral policies like single-family zoning, hindering affordable housing development in predominantly White neighborhoods and impeding racial desegregation efforts. CRT incorporates insights from sociological and literary theories that explore the intersections of political power, social organization, and language. It exerts influence across various fields, including the humanities, social sciences, and teacher education. CRT originated as a framework designed for researchers and practitioners involved in shaping public policy and addressing broader societal concerns. In response to the divisive debate around CRT and how race and racism are taught in classrooms, many states passed and introduced legislation intended to limit or ban how topics around race should be discussed.

The academic understanding of CRT differs from its representation in recent popular books and, notably, its portrayal by critics, often aligned with conservative Republicans. Detractors argue that CRT fosters negative dynamics, emphasizing group identity over shared traits, categorizing individuals into "oppressed" and "oppressor" groups, and promoting intolerance. Confusion exists regarding CRT's meaning and its relation to terms like "anti-racism" and "social justice," often conflated with it.

The term CRT is increasingly cited as the foundation for diversity and inclusion efforts, regardless of its actual influence on these programs. Some critics, like the Heritage Foundation, attribute various issues, including the 2020 Black Lives Matter protests, LGBTQ clubs in schools, diversity training in federal agencies, California's ethnic studies curriculum, free-speech debates on college campuses, and alternative disciplinary approaches, to CRT. Accusations have been made that CRT advocates for discrimination against White individuals in pursuit of equity, particularly targeting theorists like Ibram X. Kendi. As of mid-May 2022, legislation purportedly banning CRT in schools has been enacted in Idaho, Iowa, Oklahoma, and Tennessee, with similar proposals in other state legislatures.

Growing scrutiny underscores competing pressures that companies face to implement diversity initiatives and to rein them in amid conservative backlashes. For example, America First Legal and the Wisconsin Institute for Law and Liberty, two right-leaning nonprofits, have filed lawsuits in recent years against employers like Texas A&M University, Target, and Kellogg's, challenging their efforts toward diversity, equity, and inclusion, or DEI.

Some have said there is a profound psychological effect that is putting the brakes on the forward movement of diversity in the workplace. America First's complaints cite a range of hiring, promotion, and contracting programs. They include a Starbucks initiative designed to boost diversity in senior leadership and McDonald's policy of evaluating executives based in part on their efforts to diversify the company's workforce.

One of the most thought-provoking and impactful moments in the realm of racial awareness and education occurred when Jane Elliott, a renowned educator, and activist, asked a room of White individuals to stand up if they would willingly trade places with a Black person. Disturbingly, but unsurprisingly, no one stood.

Jane Elliott's simple yet profound exercise served as a powerful way to confront privilege and prejudice head-on. By challenging participants to consider the realities and systemic challenges faced by Black individuals, Elliott's approach aimed to foster empathy, self-awareness, and a deeper understanding of the inequities embedded within society. This daring action underscored the importance of recognizing one's privilege and actively working towards dismantling racial disparities, making it an indelible moment in the ongoing journey toward equality and social justice.

PART II
DISRUPTING

"We may have all come on different ships, but we're in the same boat now." – Rev. Dr. Martin Luther King, Jr.

There have been predictions that the powerful White majority will disappear in 2042. According to the Census Bureau, ethnic and racial minorities will comprise much of the population of the United States in a little more than a generation. This projection is occurring faster than anticipated just a few years ago. The United States Census Bureau calculates that by 2042, Americans who identify themselves as Hispanic, Black, Asian, American Indian, Native Hawaiian, and Pacific Islander will together outnumber non-Hispanic Whites. Four years ago, officials had projected the shift would come in 2050.

The main reason for the accelerating change is significantly higher birth rates among immigrants. Another factor is the influx of people coming into the United States, rising from about 1.3 million annually today to more than 2 million a year by midcentury, according to projections based on current immigration. These statistics have developed an environment filled with fear and for marginalized people to pay. In a fear-filled environment, even mild-mannered attempts to lead change can manifest as disruption. However, it is more important now than ever to stand as a voice of disruption focused on uniting a nation focused on division.

Implementing DEI initiatives demands more than routine measures—it requires disruption. To be effective in driving meaningful change, it is essential to embrace the role of a disruptor, challenging existing norms and dismantling barriers that hinder progress. Disruption begins with questioning the status quo. In many organizations, traditional structures and practices may perpetuate inequities. A disruptor challenges these norms, urging a critical examination of policies, hiring practices, and cultural biases that may impede diversity and inclusion.

Meaningful change often arises from uncomfortable conversations. It is almost impossible to do this work and not have consistently awkward conversations. These conversations, though challenging, pave the way for increased understanding, empathy, and awareness.

In my role as a DEI leader, my North Star was based on how I could amplify the voices of those traditionally marginalized. I spent an enormous amount of time and effort to actively seek out perspectives from individuals who may be overlooked, ensuring their experiences and insights shape the narrative. This work meant lots of meetings and conversations with anyone and everyone interested in inclusion. As nice as this sounds, I experienced heavy criticism from senior leaders and was accused of focusing on sentiment instead of strategy. I was also exhausted, as I became the person assigned to talk to every employee, who was interested in inclusion and mitigate risks stemming from exclusion.

As I often shared with skeptical senior leaders, it was my responsibility to disrupt the norm and push for structural changes within the organization. I never forget a team meeting in which I was asked to provide feedback from employees and their view of diversity within the organization. I joined the rest of the team as they were brainstorming and sharing sentiments from the employees. One of the sentiments I shared based on the numerous conversations I had with employees was that there was a culture of fear. As soon as I wrote the word fear on the whiteboard, the senior executive in the room became visibly upset. She asked me why I would note that and went on to explain how they had been working hard to change the culture and make it more welcoming to employees. After multiple conversations, the executive leader began to understand that it was my role to share the truth with employees and not to minimize the experiences of the employees. I explained that it was my goal to disrupt, and with disruption of the status quo, it was possible for change to occur.

As a DEI change agent, I worked with recruiters and managers to revise hiring practices. I helped to promote diverse leadership, which had been overlooked in the past and embedded DEI principles into the core values of the organization. I had to decide to be unafraid to challenge the fundamental structures that sustain inequity.

I often felt like I had multiple targets on my back, so I learned early on that I needed not only to build allies but also alliances. I was both successful and unsuccessful in building partnerships with like-minded individuals. In essence, being a disruptor in the realm of DEI is not about causing chaos but about dismantling structures that perpetuate inequities. It is a proactive stance that challenges the inertia of established practices, paving the way for a more inclusive and equitable future.

IV
THE PRICE TO PAY

"Prejudice is a burden that confuses the past, threatens the future, and renders the present inaccessible."
– Maya Angelou

There is definitely, most certainly, a price to pay for BIPOCs in the workplace when they get involved in DEI efforts. The cost is often too high for some to pay. In my experience, I went into the role starry-eyed and hopeful that I would be an agent of change. Over time, the level of resistance was so heavy that it created irreversible trauma.

DEI practitioners who work in organizations begin to see behavior from the C-Suite that does not match the proposed, stated values of the organization. How do we explain when we are applying for a job and at the same time asked to seek candidates that may be a better fit than ourselves? I have received numerous calls from stressed-out workers trying to understand why they are not good enough but good enough to find their replacement. DEI departments that gaslight the employees and create more trauma than do good. Comments and sentiments that are typically not shared with the general population often become common knowledge to the DEI practitioner.

At the same time, the level of *gaslighting* and the expectation to wait for an opportune time can have a debilitating impact. Gaslighting is a tactic by which a person manipulates another into questioning their reality and sanity. The purpose of gaslighting is to create an environment of confusion about what is true and what is false. Gaslighting initially manifests by eroding the DEI leader's reputation and credibility within the organization when they strive to introduce initiatives and support employees in areas that ostensibly align with the organization's values. Unfortunately, once met with resistance, the DEI leader has issues delivering on their commitments.

I remember in one of my roles, the Black ERG accused me of being a token–an Uncle Tom, an Aunt Thomasina, and an Oreo.

Looking back at all those derogatory statements, I thought them to be grossly unfair at the time. After a few years of understanding the complexities of the situation, I was unknowingly hired to placate the masses, especially People of Color. They were absolutely justified and appropriate to accuse me of being all the above. DEI practitioners are often put into situations where they are expected to control and manage the employees. Whether it is around the concept of transgender rights, abortion, or Black Lives Matter – the DEI practitioner is placed in a precarious position to manage the message and control the masses. Instead, the goal should be for senior-level executives to responsibly exert strong leadership and communication skills to convey their position around these matters. This is not the DEI person's job.

Consider the case of Malika, an African American who has a long history of solid performance within her organization. As one of the few Black people in the organization, senior leadership asks her to help with the DEI efforts. Leadership asked her in a manner that made the offer feel like a fantastic opportunity for personal and professional development. Malika is not trained in DEI strategy or privy to the history of equity within the company. Unfortunately, this is mostly never the case. In many of the situations, the person selected will often not be schooled in or familiar with African American studies and the areas of human rights, civil rights, and the like. However, because she/he is Black, they have been designated to lead the BIPOC community. This is what we have seen in the past few years as companies scramble to respond to DEI. Not only does this knee-jerk response hurt the company, but it also hurts Malika.

Consider Lamont, who has recently been selected to spearhead the DEI initiative in a non-profit organization with more than 500 employees. This was seen as an opportunity after his persistent requests for growth opportunities within the company. Despite being tasked with developing a DEI program, his leaders were not committed to providing a salary increase or a higher organizational level. Instead, they offered a nominal stipend of $25.00 for the year to lead the DEI initiative.

When Lamont shared this news, he was excited. I, on the other hand, advised him to take offense and suggested that he turn down the offer. Though he felt honored to be selected, I warned him that he was being set up for failure. After a few months, when we caught up again, Lamont revealed that the DEI efforts had failed. Several months into the position, the company concluded that he was not the ideal fit and requested him to volunteer his time in assisting them to identify someone with greater experience.

During this time, he felt his manager had started treating him differently and making comments about his DEI duties being a distraction to his work. Lamont felt that he was deliberately being pushed out by the leaders of the organization. Following that conversation, he resigned the next week. Lamont's company's response was wrong on so many levels: microaggression, showing a lack of value, a bias that infers "he should just be grateful for the opportunity," and so on.

Here is another real-life scenario and huge dilemma. Let us choose an employee from the marginalized group and have them do the DEI job. Then, the company decides to intentionally pass over the person as they look for someone with "actual experience" or someone who they feel is a better fit. Often, this person is traumatized, as they are expected to find their replacement and are constantly reminded that they are not adequate or good enough to represent the company.

Time and time again, it is reiterated to them that they are merely a temporary placeholder until they find someone more experienced, more qualified, or just plain better. There is a phenomenon that occurs in which leaders are always looking for someone better, someone who would make the senior leaders more comfortable. The solution is to have senior leadership, not the DEI person, own the risk in these initiatives. Senior leadership should be providing direction and support to the DEI practitioner. Senior leadership (CEO, COO, CFO, CHRO) should all be the guiding North Stars rather than the delegators of such important work.

THE PHENOMENON OF THE BLACK FEMALE OVERSEER

Within the evolving landscape of DEI efforts in organizations, a complex phenomenon, the Black female overseer, has emerged. This seemingly paradoxical term encapsulates a reality that demands attention, exploring the intricate interplay between representation, identity, power dynamics, and unintended consequences when individuals from diverse backgrounds are tasked with effecting change.

To grasp the paradox and implications of the Black female overseer, understanding its historical context is crucial. Rooted in a troubling legacy, the term *overseer* recalls a painful past where individuals within marginalized communities oversaw their peers' labor under oppressive conditions. In the modern workplace, it refers to a representative, often from an underrepresented group, placed in a position of authority to champion diversity and equity initiatives. Yet, these individuals may find themselves torn between advocating for change and unintentionally upholding the structures they aim to dismantle.

While superficially seen as a positive step toward diversity in leadership, complexities and pitfalls exist beneath the surface. These individuals are often chosen not solely for qualifications but also for their ethnicity or background. The organization believes that by placing them in such roles, they address diversity and fulfill a representative role. This duality, tasked with making significant change while representing one's race, forms the core of the Black female overseer paradox.

The challenge encapsulates a multifaceted dilemma, presenting individuals with a catch-22 situation. Positioned as catalysts for transformative change, they are expected to leverage their distinct perspectives to shift the organization's DEI landscape. However, instead of representing the group, they are tasked with controlling efforts and managing employees deemed overly passionate or zealous about diversity. In essence, they oversee the very groups they are supposed to support.

In my role as a diversity leader, I experienced this dynamic. Initially leading DEI, strategies driving change were implemented, and a need for an executive-level strategic partner emerged. Frustration from the executive team suggested change was happening too quickly. For instance, efforts to promote inclusivity resulted in over 5,000 employees joining employee resource groups globally. However, this influence was deemed too powerful and needed control. Conversations with other DEI leaders confirmed similar experiences of being controlled to avoid missteps.

In both instances, the individuals occupying the role of Black female overseers held positions as Chief Human Resources Officers (CHRO). The primary function of the CHRO was to establish trust and leverage it to control narratives, and employees, including myself, perpetuating harm, and trauma. I believe playing this role without giving priority to employee voices played a part in perpetuating the overseer dynamic. It is important to note that the overseer role is not restricted to being Black or female and can be interchangeable to match whichever underrepresented group requires control.

After the CHRO was hired, essential DEI efforts were paused, and every detail was scrutinized. It became evident that we were tokens controlled by a White heteronormative patriarchal narrative. Tokenism, associated with showcasing diversity without addressing systemic issues, manifested through the Black female overseer, risking relegation to a symbolic role.

The phenomenon blurs the line between advocacy and assimilation. Balancing advocating for change and assimilating into existing structures poses a challenge. Pressure to prove competence within the organization can lead to compromising core principles. In some cases, representatives unintentionally align with the structures they intend to challenge. In my case, it became clear that these CHROs acted as puppets, prompting my decision to move on.

The syndrome's crux lies in the illusion of decision-making, illustrating power dynamics. Although it seems the Black CHRO drives the slowdown of DEI initiatives, closer examination reveals decisions influenced by the CEO and C-suite leaders, excluding the individuals entrusted with DEI leadership.

The Black female overseer phenomenon embodies the interplay of representation, power dynamics, and the dangers of tokenism in DEI. To dismantle systemic inequities and foster inclusion, organizations must recognize diversity and inclusion as collective responsibilities. By acknowledging the complexities and taking comprehensive actions toward equity, organizations can transcend the paradox and create a more inclusive future.

V
AFFIRMING ACTION

"In the face of insurmountable challenges, sometimes
merely existing is a revolutionary act."
– Billy Porter

To affirm means to assert or declare something positively, with confidence and conviction. It involves expressing or confirming one's belief, support, or agreement with a particular statement, idea, or principle. Affirmation can occur in various contexts, including personal beliefs, values, opinions, commitments, or intentions. It often involves expressing confidence, trust, and positivity, either towards oneself or towards others. Affirmation can be verbal or written, and it serves to reinforce or validate a particular viewpoint or position. It can also be used as a form of encouragement, self-motivation, or self-improvement by emphasizing positive thoughts, qualities, or aspirations. The root word "affirm" means to state or declare something positively or firmly, often to assert its truth or validity. It can also signify the act of confirming or supporting a belief, statement, or proposition.

THE COST OF AFFIRMATIVE ACTION

Diversity is being defunded as individuals ease off and retract their commitment to it. In Natasha Bowman's article, 'DEI= Dead End Initiatives,' she acknowledges that organizational efforts to eliminate systemic racism in the workplace are increasingly becoming performative, lacking accountability, and destined to fail. DEI efforts in the workplace are currently on life support, with minimal chances of survival. Let's examine why DEI roles are disappearing faster than non-DEI roles.

A recently published article stated, "DEI roles increased by 55% following demands for broader racial equity and justice after [George] Floyd's murder." However, three years later, as the economy churns, these roles disappear faster than non-DEI roles. I predicted this would happen as these roles and departments were created without giving these leaders budgets, autonomy, or commitment from leaders in non-DEI positions.

With theories and unfounded speculations like the examples above, affirmative action remains vulnerable. Affirmative action refers to policies and practices aimed at promoting equal opportunities for historically marginalized groups, such as women, racial and ethnic minorities, and individuals with disabilities. While the impact of affirmative action on corporations can vary depending on specific circumstances and implementation, it generally affects them in various ways.

Affirmative action encourages corporations to actively seek and hire individuals from underrepresented groups. This can lead to a more diverse workforce, which has been linked to various benefits, including increased innovation, improved problem-solving, and enhanced creativity. By expanding the talent pool and providing opportunities to a broader range of individuals, corporations can tap into a more comprehensive range of perspectives and experiences.

To comply with affirmative action requirements, corporations often implement strategies to reach out to and attract candidates from underrepresented groups. This may involve targeted recruitment efforts, partnerships with organizations that serve diverse communities, and the establishment of diversity and inclusion programs. By broadening their recruitment practices, companies can increase the chances of hiring qualified individuals from marginalized backgrounds. Affirmative action policies aim to address historical disadvantages and promote equal opportunities. By actively considering candidates from underrepresented groups, corporations can help reduce systemic barriers and provide a more level playing field. This fosters a sense of fairness and promotes equal access to opportunities within the organization. In some districts, corporations may be legally required to implement affirmative action policies.

Compliance with these regulations ensures that companies do not engage in discriminatory practices and promotes equality in the workplace. By adhering to these policies, corporations mitigate the risk of legal action and potential reputational damage. Affirmative action can stimulate cultural shifts within corporations. By embracing diversity and inclusion, organizations can create an environment where employees from different backgrounds feel valued and empowered. This can lead to improved employee morale, increased productivity, and a more inclusive organizational culture.

Demonstrating a commitment to diversity and inclusion through affirmative action can positively impact a corporation's reputation. Consumers and stakeholders often expect companies to reflect the diversity of the communities they serve. By actively promoting diversity, corporations can enhance their brand image and attract customers who value inclusive practices. It is important to note that the specific effects of affirmative action on corporations can vary depending on the context, industry, and how policies are implemented. Additionally, affirmative action remains a topic of debate, with differing opinions on its efficacy and potential unintended consequences.

BLACK LIVES MATTER

The murder of George Floyd was a catalyst for many organizations to start or reevaluate their Diversity, Equity, and Inclusion initiatives. Floyd's murder led to widespread protests and increased public awareness of systemic racism and police brutality. This increased awareness led many organizations to reflect upon and revise their policies and practices related to diversity, equity, and inclusion. As such, many employees called on their employers to act and implement these DEI initiatives following George Floyd's murder. This pressure came from employees affected by racial inequality and allies who wanted to support their colleagues and create a more inclusive workplace culture. Many of these "allies" that were once posting Black Lives Matter have forgotten that systemic racism against Black Americans ignited this movement and are now claiming that these efforts were not centered around the Black experience at work.

It pains me to say this, but the recent actions of organizations and allies have shown that we have returned to the pre-COVID era of being unseen, unheard, and undervalued at work and in the community. The failed efforts of organizations to make good on their DEI promises and the backpedaling of White allies are dangerous and can lead to several negative consequences. The most dangerous of these consequences is the impact on the mental health of its Black employees. When DEI commitments fail, Black employees may feel devalued and excluded from the workplace. This can lead to feelings of isolation, anxiety, and depression and can negatively impact mental health.

Failed DEI commitments can contribute to imposter syndrome, which is the feeling of being a fraud or not deserving of success. Black employees may feel like they are not valued or appreciated for their contributions to the workplace, which can lead to feelings of self-doubt and anxiety. Failed DEI commitments can erode trust and safety in the workplace, which can negatively impact mental health. Black employees may feel they cannot speak up about their concerns or experiences without fear of retaliation or dismissal.

Black employees may experience secondary trauma due to ongoing racial discrimination and inequality in the workplace. This can also and concurrently lead to feelings of hopelessness, anger, and despair and can negatively impact mental health.

Failed DEI commitments can significantly impact the mental health of Black employees, leading to feelings of devaluation, stress, burnout, imposter syndrome, lack of trust and safety, and secondary trauma. Organizations must prioritize effective DEI initiatives to create a more inclusive and equitable workplace culture supporting all employees' mental health and well-being.

Hush Money: How One Woman Proved Systemic Racism in Her Workplace and Kept Her Job, by Jacquie Abram recounts the true story of a Black woman who, in the face of injustice, experienced profound emotional distress. The book explores her traumatic workplace experiences and offers strategies for navigating similar challenges. The book addresses overt racism infiltrating organizations, revealing what they currently overlook. Through the story of a fictional character, Ebony, it explores her encounters working with a racist figure in higher education.

I personally related to Ebony and her not just one racist but multiple co-players, including her boss, co-workers, and even human resources. The stress and toll on Ebony while going through her own physical and mental health challenges and family challenges. HR and her boss are simultaneously gossiping and setting it up so she will be fired when she returns. It reminded me of a time when I was so stressed in my DEI work that I nearly bled to death as stress caused me to hemorrhage at work. Instead of going home, I rinsed my blood-stained clothes out in the bathroom and dried them with the dryer to prepare for the next DEI presentation that I had later that day.

The real-life racial discrimination, retaliation, and racially based preferred treatment of Whites and other employees is real. Often DEI leaders wait until we attend conferences and other private moments before we discuss the discriminatory events that have occurred that cause us nervousness, anxiety, night terrors, panic attacks, and loss of sleep. The DEI role often uncovers those covert strategies that workplace oppressors employ.

The conniving whispers in the hallways, the calculated exclusion from meetings, the thinly veiled threats disguised as jokes. Each instance created a thread in the intricate web of betrayal that is often spun around marginalized communities.

I have experienced those interactions with co-workers. Our interactions transformed from cordial exchanges to icy glares and hushed conversations the moment I dared to challenge the *status quo*. And people just simply avoiding me and any affiliation to DEI work.

VI
THE LIES & THE TRUTH ABOUT IMPOSTER SYNDROME

"Our labor historically has been used to make the lives of White women less hectic and more relaxed."
– Tricia Hersey

THE IMPOSTER SYNDROME LIE

Psychologists Pauline R. Clance and Suzanne A. Imes coined the term *imposter syndrome* in 1978. It describes an internal experience where individuals, despite evidence of high achievement, believe they are not intelligent, capable, or creative. In essence, imposter syndrome manifests as an internal voice undermining your abilities, incessantly whispering that you fall short and are merely a facade on the brink of exposure.

The reality is as a Black woman I was much less likely than my non-Black colleagues to interact with senior leaders at work. I struggled with this lack of access when finding sponsorship. I literally did not expect support and believed the onus was completely on me to advance my career.

I now know that Black women are less likely to be included in essential conversations about company priorities and strategy. We have fewer opportunities to get noticed by people in leadership. Imposter syndrome is that feeling that you do not belong here, wherever "here" is for you: the office, your friend group, the classroom, or the board- room. It does not matter how qualified you are, how much experience you have, or how much reassurance and positive feedback you may receive. With imposter syndrome, you cannot shake the notion that you are just not as capable as others may believe you are, and therefore, you are doomed for failure.

An estimated 70% of Americans struggle with these intrusive thoughts brought on by imposter syndrome. And while imposter syndrome is not a diagnosable condition, it can result in adverse mental health outcomes. Mental health experts believe that prolonged feelings of isolation and stress brought on by the phenomenon can lead to other illnesses, such as anxiety and depression. People of Color are particularly vulnerable to this debilitating sensation. That is because, for us, imposter syndrome is not just an imaginary voice in our heads. It can be heard loud and clear when we receive almost daily messages from society that we truly do not belong.

This feeling of otherness is a common occurrence in the workplace where, too often, we may be the only person of color present. It happens in stores when we are stalked by security when shopping. It occurs every time we turn on the TV, open a book, or watch a movie and do not see anyone who looks like us doing anything besides being a sidekick.

The world—subliminally and outright—tells us that we do not belong, that we are not good enough.

Imposter syndrome has become a part of life for many People of Color, but that does not have to be the case. We can battle the phenomenon and discrimination simply by continuing to show up. Increasing our representation in the places that have historically excluded us benefits the institutions and creates an environment where we no longer feel like outliers. Simply, the more of us in the room, the more we will feel like we belong there and the less alone we will feel in our minds. But it is not solely our responsibility to combat this.

The ugly cousin of imposter syndrome is the lie of executive presence. This is very personal to me. For years, it was insinuated in my corporate jobs that I lacked executive presence. Between the assumed lack of executive presence and the lack of politicking, it was assumed that others and I needed to be more capable of playing in the big league, the C-suite. Digging into this dilemma and ultimate lie, we can pinpoint this practice to the measure of progress by standards built in White supremacy. Other actions include changing the way we think about work. The term "professionalism," rooted in a White, heteronormative perspective of what is considered professional, has also posed challenges.

The definition of professionalism needs a makeover. Professionalism is based on the United States' middle and upper-class values and European ideals of appearance. We also need to revisit and maintain a laser focus on the view of women in the workplace. Although women have made significant strides over the last 100 years, COVID-19 has reminded us of the occupational segregation that persists in the workplace. Women continue to bear the responsibility of managing the home. Many women, specifically women of color, are in the jobs that stand up for the rest of the economy — childcare, elder care, and care for disabled folks. The dilemma is the lack of job protection for those who care for others due to stringent corporate policies that do not allow flexibility for caregivers. We lack specific policies that we know will contribute to gender, racial, and economic justice.

The lack of certain provisions has perpetuated and exacerbated racial, gender, and economic inequality. These include the absence of paid leave, inadequate, inaccessible, and unaffordable childcare, as well as the same deficiencies in elder care and gaps in unemployment insurance. It is crucial to pay attention to how the absence of these elements has significantly contributed to racial, gender, and economic inequality. In 2021, women's labor force participation was at the level of 30 years ago. There are 4 million fewer women in the workforce today than just a year ago. The situation is a lot more dire for African-American and Hispanic women than what is happening for White women. Researchers have found that about 80% of White Americans hold unconscious biases against marginalized persons. That is because most Americans are exposed to negative stereotypes about Black and Brown people.

These biases occur instantaneously that they kick in before a person can process them. The messaging is so pervasive in America that a third of Black Americans hold anti-Black bias against themselves.

THE TRUTH

Throughout my career, the color of my skin felt like an invisible cloak. Early in my career, I would let others speak for me and forfeit my voice. I remember a humiliating moment when a White woman felt the need to teach my name to other people in the room. We often face the perception of ingratitude when we speak up or challenge how we are treated. Strangely, others become uncomfortable when marginalized groups empower themselves. It is crucial that we foster our empowerment through economic means.

Marcus Garvey was the founder of the Universal Negro Improvement Association (UNIA). Formed in Jamaica in July 1914, the UNIA aimed to achieve Black nationalism through the celebration of African history and culture. It was on point and on track, a visionary ahead of his time with his back-to-Africa philosophies and movement. Today, it is *en vogue* to go back to Africa, be Afrocentric, etc. As much as they did not want us here, they could not afford our free labor to leave either.

We also need to free ourselves from the White gaze that Toni Morrison wrote so eloquently about. The "Pet to Threat" phenomenon reflects one aspect of a host of implicit and systemic biases that too often derail the careers of talented People of Color. Pet to threat is another dilemma and occurrence in the workplace that occurs when People of Color are no longer seen as a novelty but have now become viewed as a threat when we exhibit assertiveness or any form of ambition.

Then, there is the phenomenon that occurs when Black women injure and harm other women and women of color in the workplace. Many believe that this behavior originates from the plantation when scarcity drove our needs to survive in the Black community. We have learned not to gather or commune. Black people and other marginalized groups have learned to stay in our lane and under the radar.

Most recently, a friend of mine posted a professional photo on LinkedIn with an insightful and engaging caption. In the photo, she had on a fitted dress and was leaning, so all of her curves were showing, no skin, just curves. After receiving comments like "she was selling sex" to promote her consulting business, she and I discussed and agreed wholeheartedly this was just another example of the double standard that Black women face when celebrating ourselves and our bodies. Women, in general, have been sexualized in this country, judged by our bodies, and body shamed.

In an attempt to fit in, we have covered our skin color, hair texture, and our curves. We have suppressed our beauty and brains for the fear and shame that comes from the White gaze. Knowing that because of our skin color and position in this country, we could be exploited without recourse or justice. One of the most egregious and insidious actions occurs when women of color are used as tokens to create safe spaces for other women by exploiting their experiences.

A recent article spoke about a Black woman recruited to be an executive coach assigned to facilitate group sessions and their members. In the orientation, the first icebreaker included sharing your "spirit animal." The new executive coach was immediately anxious about the increasing internal alarm as the group of predominantly White women executive coaches went around the room and participated in this activity. When they got to her, she was nervous. Still, she introduced herself and said that as a non-Indigenous, non-Native person, she could not participate in that part of the exercise, as she felt it was cultural appropriation and a form of obliteration. Awkwardly, the coach that followed, the only other women of color coach there, said something in defense of the exercise. Then everything proceeded around the table, "business as usual," minimizing and ignoring the statement about appropriation. Later on, the facilitator spoke with the new executive coach about their concern about being an executive coach, mainly due to others in the group who have viewpoints she might find problematic and who might feel judged by her.

Due to this expression of truth, sharing her identity and beliefs in a group designed for equity that she thought was safe, she was never assigned a group or a role in a group. After a few months, the new executive coach "resigned" so that she would not have to keep getting their emails asking her to fill out the schedule for availability and receiving no response. It is this White supremacy-based culture that has responded and perpetuated the feelings of imposter syndrome, insecurity, and shame when we show up as our honest and vulnerable selves.

PART III
DECIDING

"If we cannot now end our differences, at least we can help make the world safe for diversity."
– John F. Kennedy

As described in Chapter 5, Dead End Initiatives –the acronym that shares the same letters as DEI, can occur in human resource departments that are not suitably empowered. HR often does not allow a safe place for DEI to sit.

Putting people in place without a strategy quickly becomes worrisome for anyone, leading to failure and burnout. DEI initiatives are vital for creating inclusive and equitable workplaces. However, some arguments have been made against DEI being solely housed within HR. Some reasons include having a limited focus. That is, placing DEI solely within HR can limit its scope and effectiveness.

HR departments traditionally focus on compliance, policies, and procedures, which may not fully address the broader cultural and systemic issues related to diversity and inclusion. DEI should be a strategic priority that involves all levels of an organization, not just HR. Another issue is tokenization and symbolism. If DEI initiatives are confined to HR, they may be seen as merely symbolic gestures or checkboxes to fulfill legal or public relations obligations. This perception can undermine the credibility and impact of these initiatives. DEI efforts should be integrated throughout the organization to foster genuine cultural change.

VII
DIE IN HR DEI

"Our ability to reach unity in diversity will be the beauty
and the test of our civilization."
— Mahatma Gandhi

HR professionals, including myself, navigate a complex landscape where the pursuit of justice and equity often intersects with organizational politics and interests. While the core objective of HR is to foster a harmonious and inclusive work environment, the reality can be more nuanced. Indeed, there are instances where HR is inadvertently incentivized to overlook or manage discrimination cases in ways that prioritize the company's reputation or financial stability.

Yet, amidst these challenges, there exists a profound sense of fulfillment for HR practitioners who choose to champion marginalized employees and advocate for their rights. Being a beacon of support and a resource for individuals who face discrimination can be deeply rewarding. The ability to offer guidance, empathy, and tangible solutions can make a significant impact on the lives of those who have felt silenced or marginalized within their workplace.

Unfortunately, in organizations tainted by racism or bias, HR's role can indeed be reduced to that of a minion. Employees, desperate for resolution, often turn to HR as a last resort, believing that their concerns will be met with empathy and action. Regrettably, HR can sometimes find itself caught in a challenging position where the pressure to protect the company's interests conflicts with the obligation to uphold ethical and legal standards.

The concept of HR acting as minions underscores the systemic challenges within organizations that fail to prioritize equity and inclusion. However, it is crucial to acknowledge that not all HR professionals fall into this category. Many HR individuals recognize the importance of professional courage—the determination to navigate challenging circumstances with integrity. This courage involves standing up against discriminatory practices, engaging in uncomfortable conversations with leadership, and pushing for meaningful change, even when met with resistance.

In a broader sense, the narrative surrounding HR's role reflects the multifaceted nature of workplace dynamics. It is a reminder that HR can be a force for positive change when guided by values of justice, empathy, and equity. The call to action for HR professionals is to rise above the pitfalls of complicity and instead strive to be advocates for those who need their support the most, ultimately contributing to the transformation of workplaces into spaces where every employee's voice is heard and respected.

By separating DEI from HR, there can be a more apparent distinction between the roles and responsibilities. Placing DEI under a different department or creating a dedicated

DEI team allows for better accountability and authority to drive change. It ensures that DEI is kept from HR's primary functions or relegated to a secondary concern.

DEI is everyone's responsibility within an organization, not just HR's. Placing it solely within HR can create a perception that DEI is solely an HR issue, leading others to disengage from the process. By involving employees from various departments and levels, organizations can foster broader ownership and collaboration, making DEI initiatives more effective.

DEI is not just about training or hiring practices; it often requires challenging existing structures and systems that perpetuate inequities. Placing DEI solely within HR may not provide the authority or influence needed to drive significant structural changes. Integrating DEI into various departments and leadership roles can help ensure that the necessary changes are implemented across the organization. It is important to note that these arguments are not against DEI itself but rather about the best way to implement and support DEI initiatives within organizations. The specific structure and approach will vary depending on the organization's size, culture, and industry.

I would like to share my actual resignation letter from a head of DEI role that left me exhausted, enraged, and more enraged:

Dear CEO & CHRO

Please accept this formal statement regarding my resignation from the position of DEI Manager with (Company). My last day was today (Date).

I accepted the role excited about the opportunity to support the DEI initiative at (Company). During my time in the position, I have used my skills and experience to establish a foundation around DEI at (Company) that will remain my legacy. However, recently, the level of psychological safety I have attempted to create for employees I could not achieve for myself. For example, my employee experience while applying for the newly created Director of DEI role felt devaluing, disrespectful, and demoralizing. In short, the recent lack of support for my role and my overall employee experience was causing a strain on my physical, emotional, and mental well-being.

With that said, I am proud of the following achievements:

- *Paving the way and impacting sustainable change for our company.*
- *Developing content to communicate our corporate social responsibility (CSR) work and DEI initiatives to support various awards and recognitions.*
- *Maintaining platforms for learning and courageous conversations through panel discussions and monthly celebrations.*
- *Partnering with various employee groups to ensure employee voices were heard.*
- *Creating mentoring programs within the business to strengthen our talent pipeline and the continued integration of our DEI and culture strategies.*

Developing and empowering my peers to support the business with skills and abilities that would continue and sustain DEI work.

To follow are areas of opportunities that I share in the hopes that this may help (the organization) develop an authentic, equitable, and inclusive culture:

- *Avoid tasking DEI leaders to solve every imaginable DEI problem with minimal resources. (i.e., instead of two people dedicated to DEI to serve 15,000 employees globally, provide funding and staff able to stand up a viable initiative.)*
- *Develop a senior DEI leadership role that will report directly to the C-suite. In this work, like optics, titles matter.*
- *Provide a realistic budget and autonomy around budgeting decisions comparable to other senior leaders.*
- *Avoid devaluing and viewing DEI as "peripheral" to the core business of the organization.*
- *Invest in transformative change and not performative actions.*
- *Protect DEI leaders from being burned out by the workload, constant attacks and pushback against their work, and the lack of support.*
- *Provide transparency around data internally and externally.*
- *Be authentic and deliberate in terms of initiatives. (i.e., recognition of cultural holidays, mentorship programs, and support of employee resource groups as a part of the overall business strategy).*
- *Respond with urgency to employee relations issues involving protected classes.*
- *Prioritize the development of HR & employee relations professionals trained in mediating and identifying potential discrimination claims.*

As the third DEI person in this position who has remained in the role for less than two years, I wish the organization success in finding a DEI leader who will stay the course.

I felt an imperative to provide such an in-depth resignation addressed to the organization's top leaders, not just out of obligation, but out of a profound sense of responsibility. Like many leaders, I embarked on DEI initiatives with enthusiasm and a vision of leaving a lasting impact. This letter serves as a personal reminder that I fulfilled my commitment. It is crucial for the organization to recognize the need for improvement. Moreover, I want to affirm to myself and immortalize this moment in history, acknowledging that I exerted my utmost effort.

Have you ever attempted to swim against a strong current? Whether it is in a river, ocean, or even a pool. As you reach the middle, you begin to sense the force pushing back and doubt your decision to be able to successfully complete the effort. It is a situation to which we can all relate. This is how I felt when I was called to lead DEI in various organizations. It felt as if I was pushing something that felt like it was almost pushing back. It felt impossible at times. I share this analogy because doing DEI work may leave you feeling like you are being pushed while, at the same time, being pulled.

This entire book delves into these challenges, triumphs, and revelations experienced during my journey to foster diversity, equity, and inclusion within the organization. At the heart of my story is my genuine excitement and honor when accepting the role to lead DEI for the organization. I was deeply committed to cultivating an inclusive workplace, and I continue to hold a deep belief in creating a legacy of positive change. However, a year into my role, the narrative took an unexpected turn as I grappled with the stark realization that the psychological safety, I sought to create for employees remained elusive for myself.

My personal experiences, including a degrading application process for a Director of DEI role, exemplified the internal struggle I faced. The conflicting emotions, feelings of devaluation, and a lack of support compelled me to resign.

Amidst my decision, I attempted to highlight the achievements that I was proud of, hoping to pave the way for sustainable transformation, initiating vital conversations through platforms, partnering with employee groups, and empowering peers to champion DEI efforts.

My goal is to shed light on the intricacies of managing DEI initiatives within a corporate environment. I want to articulate vital areas of opportunity for organizations to develop a truly inclusive culture, addressing critical issues like resource allocation, budgeting, senior leadership roles, and the importance of authentic, transformative actions over superficial gestures.

Window dressing and performative DEI efforts can result in the retention of diverse employees becoming challenging. When employees feel that their voices and contributions are not genuinely valued, they are more likely to leave the organization in search of a workplace that genuinely supports their growth and development. High turnover rates can be costly for organizations and disrupt team dynamics.

It is essential to be on the lookout for missed opportunities for growth. Authentic DEI efforts can lead to improved decision-making and enhanced problem-solving capabilities. However, when organizations focus on the appearance of diversity rather than the substance, they miss the benefits that come from diverse perspectives and experiences. This can hinder the organization's ability to innovate and adapt to changing markets. Externally, window dressing and performative DEI can damage the organization's reputation. With increased scrutiny from customers, clients, and the public, organizations that are not genuinely committed to diversity and inclusion can face backlash and boycotts. A negative reputation can not only impact but destroy the company's bottom line and market standing.

By focusing on superficial diversity, organizations may need to address systemic inequalities and biases that affect marginalized groups. This can perpetuate existing disparities and prevent meaningful progress toward creating an inclusive workplace where everyone has equitable opportunities, widening inequality instead of bridging the gap. To foster a truly inclusive workplace and mitigate these negative consequences, organizations should commit to authentic DEI efforts. This involves comprehensive assessments of policies, practices, and culture, followed by strategic initiatives that promote equitable representation, belonging, and respect for all employees, regardless of their background. Window dressing can increase the brand but be performative.

DEI should not be confused with cultural work to make everyone feel good but should be focused on removing biases. A recent Gartner research study found that 42% of employees report that their peers view their organization's DEI efforts as divisive. Another 42% say that their peers resent DEI efforts altogether. These types of feelings can serve as a gateway for pushback behavior. In their work, Gartner has identified three forms of pushback and how they show up in the workplace. They are denial, disengagement, and derailment.

Denial refers to the belief that there is no issue at hand. It occurs when workers fail to recognize the presence of social constructs such as race, class, or caste, overlook instances of discrimination and prejudice, and neglect to explore the reasons behind the underrepresentation of marginalized groups in the workplace.

Disengagement is the notion that this is not my problem. Typically, individuals who disengage are conscious of the existence of systemic disparities but choose not to endorse or take part in DEI initiatives. This can stem from different motives, such as a concern about making mistakes and inadvertently causing harm or a general reluctance to get involved.

Lastly, there is the concept of derailment. This refers to the act of questioning, *What about other issues?* Derailment involves trying to disregard the concerns of marginalized groups, overlooking the problems that DEI initiatives aim to tackle, and shifting attention back to dominant groups. Throughout my professional journey, I collaborated with organizations that faced challenges in effectively involving leaders who needed to be more open to embracing change.

There are various strategies that can be used when there is a feeling that you may be involved in active derailment. The first step is to take a pause and assess how the push-back is affecting your well-being. It is essential to take a conscious moment of reflection that serves as a reminder to listen to learn versus developing a counterargument. In fact, developing counterarguments is counter to your well-being. Let me explain.

Developing counterarguments, in and of themselves, are not inherently detrimental to your well-being. In fact, the use of them can be a valuable skill that promotes critical thinking and helps you engage in meaningful discussions. However, there are a few ways in which developing counterarguments may have adverse effects on your well-being. Constantly engaging in counter argumentation can lead to overthinking and heightened stress levels. If you find yourself continually analyzing and dissecting every idea or statement, it can become mentally exhausting and detrimental to your overall well-being. While healthy debates and discussions can be intellectually stimulating, developing counterarguments without considering the impact on interpersonal relationships can strain connections. If you are constantly challenging and opposing others, it may create tension, hostility, and damaged relationships.

If you frequently focus on counterarguments, it can contribute to a negative mindset, cynicism, and a tendency to view situations from a skeptical or cynical perspective. This can hinder your ability to appreciate positive aspects, develop trust, or engage in constructive problem-solving. Dealing with negative and alternative views around disability without the ability to accept alternative viewpoints can allow you to constantly develop counterarguments, making it challenging for you to genuinely consider alternative perspectives or be open to new ideas. This framework can lead to a closed-minded approach, limiting personal growth and preventing the ability to learn from others.

Another consequence is emotional exhaustion. Engaging in counter argumentation can be emotionally draining, especially when topics are extremely sensitive or personal. Constantly challenging others' beliefs or defending your own can evoke strong emotions and create a sense of exhaustion, impacting your overall emotional well-being.

To maintain a balance, it is essential to recognize when and where to apply counter argumentation appropriately. It is valuable to develop critical thinking skills. Still, it is equally important to cultivate empathy, understanding, and the ability to engage in constructive dialogue that fosters mutual respect and growth.

When I started in DEI, I felt I could use my critical skills, debate experience, influence, and the art of persuasion to win people over to a commitment to DEI. I was sorely disappointed by the fact that a large percentage of the employee base, especially leaders, needed to be convinced that DEI was an important initiative to help them reach their current goals. When asked, they would agree that it was necessary, but their actions did not match their words—which frequently felt personal and discouraging.

It is important to remember that we all come to every interaction undeniably informed by our past experiences and underlying biases and assumptions. Accepting that allows us to consciously adjust our mindsets and behaviors and actively decide to engage with new perspectives. Staying focused on your purpose and your personal commitment toward a common goal is vital.

As an inclusivity leader, you will need to move with professional courage as you step into conversations and prioritize pushback with empathy and clarity of purpose. Although it is easy to say that change always comes with resistance, it is challenging to face resistance every day as you attempt to meet primary DEI goals. As you begin to assess the current state of pushback in your organization, remember your goal is to change systems, not people. To do work with people, not for them. Ultimately, organizations committed to promoting diversity, equity, and inclusion must choose to persist in their efforts, even when faced with challenges and adversity that may seem insurmountable.

RATIONING RESOURCES

In a recent piece by DEI Advisor, Taylor Odisho, it is affirmed that Chief Diversity Officers (CDOs) require sufficient resources and a realistic time frame to bring about lasting cultural change. For effective diversity initiatives, the C-suite must actively engage with and support these efforts. Three key methods involve allocating ample budgets, endorsing ERGs, and integrating DEI into the overall business strategy. To mitigate burnout, a significant factor contributing to high turnover, CDOs must prioritize self-care and acknowledge that the work will persist. According to an analysis by Russell Reynolds Associates on S&P 500 CDOs, the average tenure of chief diversity officers is currently a mere 1.8 years. This highlights a recurring diversity challenge: both novice and experienced CDOs, regardless of their level of expertise and enthusiasm, tend to have relatively short tenures.

According to a recent LinkedIn analysis of C-suite hiring trends, Chief Diversity and Inclusion Officers experienced a substantial 168.9% increase in hires from 2019 to 2021. Despite a slight decline of 4.5% in 2022, the Korn Ferry Survey of Professionals found that 78% of respondents considered CDOs more crucial in 2022 than in the summer of 2020. While there are many opportunities for diversity leaders to transition to organizations with stronger dedication and better resources for supporting DEI initiatives, it is emphasized that a company's commitment to diversity and inclusion should not solely rely on the presence of a CDO. Before appointing a Chief Diversity Officer, the C-suite, management, and board of directors should clearly understand why DEI is a priority and determine how the organization plans to integrate it into its overall strategy. By making DEI a collective effort rather than placing the entire responsibility on one person, there is a potential for a stronger synergy between the organization and its workforce. It is suggested that, as a prospective diversity leader, one should assess an organization's commitment to DEI during the interview process, ensuring alignment before accepting the role.

EMPLOYEE RESOURCE GROUPS (ERGs)

Often, the very strategy to empower an organization can create a toxic environment of segregation and degradation. I have witnessed the creation of employee resource groups as a performative tactic and not a strategic act of inclusion. Please do not get me wrong. I understand the power of ERGs.

However, there are serious pitfalls that can occur when developing these groups if done incorrectly, with minimal support and resources. Employee resource groups can provide many benefits to organizations and employees, but they can also have potential negatives and pitfalls. Here are a few:

> Lack of inclusion: ERGs may unintentionally create divisions within the organization by focusing on specific identities or groups. This could lead to exclusion or feelings of marginalization among employees who do not identify with the group's focus. It is essential to ensure that ERGs are inclusive and considerate of all employees' needs.
>
> Tokenism: Sometimes, ERGs can be seen as a way for organizations to appear diverse and inclusive without genuinely addressing systemic issues. Suppose ERGs are perceived as a mere checkbox exercise or a way to «tick off» diversity goals without meaningful action. In that case, it can lead to feelings of tokenism among members and undermine the credibility of these groups.
>
> Limited impact: ERGs can become siloed within organizations, only focusing on their specific issues and failing to create systemic change or address broader diversity and inclusion challenges. To be effective, ERGs should collaborate with other departments, leadership, and HR teams to address systemic issues and implement meaningful change.
>
> Burnout and overrepresentation: ERG members often take on additional responsibilities outside of their regular job roles to support the group initiatives. This can lead to burnout and overburdening of individuals who

are already underrepresented or marginalized within the organization.

Reinforcing stereotypes: If ERGs unintentionally reinforce stereotypes or inadvertently create a perception of segregation, it can hinder progress toward true inclusivity. Organizations should foster an environment where ERGs work towards breaking down barriers rather than perpetuating them.

Limited resources and support: ERGs may need help in obtaining sufficient resources, minimal budgets, and support from the organization. This lack of resources can hinder their ability to achieve their objectives and impact change effectively.

Participants who speak up about DEI injustices in the workplace are often seen as activists and troublemakers. Employees do not always have the political correctness or emotional maturity to express their dissatisfaction with the state of DEI. They often are seen by leaders as divisive or just too loud and disruptive.

Employees may be shunned, ostracized, or demoted, as I have personally witnessed on many occasions. This phenomenon has been personally troubling to me, as I have personally recruited employees to participate in or lead ERGs, only to see them become frustrated and labeled by senior leaders. They retain labels like ineffective, incompetent, and poor performers based on their decision to be vulnerable and vocal in the ERGs. This is one of the most problematic consequences that I have had the misfortune to manage as a DEI leader.

To any of those employees who have served on ERGs under my leadership, I apologize for pulling you into groups for whom the organization was not ready. I apologize for causing you unnecessary hurt and trauma and affecting your ability to grow within the organization.

One situation close to home is the story of Melissa and the decline in her career after deciding to become the leader of a women's group. Collectively, Melissa and a few women spearheading the group chose to name the group 'Empower.' The senior leaders immediately expressed dissatisfaction with the group, who was leading the group, and the name of the group. The organization's reluctance to have a junior female leader at the forefront of the group stemmed from a perceived disparity in experience and perhaps an underlying bias. Despite the fact that the group was initiated by a few junior leaders, there was a resistance to allowing a junior female to take a leading role. The use of the term "empower" was viewed as condescending by the organization, indicating a sensitivity to language that may unintentionally diminish the capabilities or authority of those being empowered. Interestingly, the contradiction arises from the fact that the group was founded by junior leaders, suggesting a grassroots initiative driven by individuals who might bring fresh perspectives and innovative ideas. However, the organization's preference for prominent, visible, and all-White senior leaders to lead the group implies a resistance to deviating from traditional power structures and an inclination towards maintaining the status quo.

This situation highlights the tension between established hierarchies and the potential for diversity and inclusion within organizational leadership. It prompts a reflection on whether the organization may be missing valuable contributions by not embracing a more diverse leadership approach. Additionally, the discomfort with the term "empower" raises questions about the organization's understanding of fostering an inclusive and supportive environment.

Organizations must be mindful of these potential pitfalls and take proactive steps to address them. Regular assessment, open communication, and collaboration with ERGs can help mitigate these negatives and ensure their positive impact on the organization's overall diversity and inclusion efforts.

The organization's resources need to be improved, and diverse leaders must be left alone to effect change. Just like other C-suite roles, CDOs require a budget that allows them to build out employee resource groups, hire employees to collect and analyze data and create partnerships with professional organizations. During the implementation phase, it becomes crucial to have the necessary resources and personnel in place. This includes administrative assistants, project managers, individuals managing employee resource groups, and those aiding in learning and development.

A larger budget also leads to better data, from collecting it to interpreting it. For example, you may have a DEI team that includes a people analytics role dedicated to tracking the organization's progress and predictive analytics to understand where they need to adjust. Organizations that have successfully mastered the skills of dissecting and analyzing data are more advanced compared to their peers.

Big data assists with putting some rigor around diversity and helps to legitimize it among peers. With this data, leaders and organizations become more satisfied. It is important that DEI does not rely solely on anecdotes, but rather, areas for improvement should be clearly identified. However, collecting and synthesizing this data takes time and patience, which is not a luxury or privilege freely given to DEI leaders. Causing yet another dilemma.

For example, GE Appliances used data to set a goal to reach 40% women and 40% People of Color in its employee makeup to better reflect its consumers. They did this because they knew diversity would make us a more innovative and competitive business. This goal drove the need for better data analytics and a more strategic approach to attracting, developing, engaging, and retaining talent. The organization also saw a need to better understand the impact of bias, which led to new practices, such as more diverse slates for open roles and diverse interview panels to optimize the playing field. The organization also looked at retention trends by function and implemented strategies and tactics to drive improvement.

Often, the C-suite has unrealistic expectations for DEI progress; cultural change requires time in addition to money. There is a perception that organizational culture change takes a long time, longer than the tenure of a leader, longer than the attention span of the organization—so long that other high-priority initiatives will, by necessity, distract the organization from completing the effort. For example, organizations that treat diversity objectives with the same timeline as financial ones will see better results and a happier CDO.

For example, DEI leaders should have the same access and technological tools that other teams have to communicate DEI outcomes. Like other leaders, those leading DEI are driven to succeed and aspire to witness tangible progress in those metrics. DEI leaders should also review key performance indicators and other outcome analyses to assess the impact and identify areas that require reworking.

C-level executives need to be more engaged with diversity initiatives. Often, fellow C-level executives need to be more engaged with diversity initiatives. Frankly speaking, my experience had been that the other C-suite leaders did not have my back. Often, it felt like they were rooting for my failure. Like any other employee, support is essential for CDOs to feel motivated. They have to understand the intentionality of the support. This means that C-suite members are sponsoring ERGs, attending DEI workshops, and leading difficult conversations that drive the diversity mission. The work does not end when a CDO is hired.

When CDOs work in partnership with other members of the C-suite, the DEI initiatives gain more traction. Trust is developed by having honest conversations. Relaying goals and strategies for changing company culture shows how diversity helps the bottom line. Although challenging, leaders must step away from the urge to be competitive and realize that everyone is on the journey together.

Many organizations are taking commitment a step further by requiring inclusive leadership training. On the other hand, organizations approach DEI as a nice-to-have and not a requirement or mandatory initiative.

When organizations are committed to having leaders participate in training, such as inclusive leadership that looks at self-awareness, it takes on several personas. It will look like vulnerability; it will entail talking with our leaders about empathy, compassion, curiosity, accountability, and all the pieces that will ultimately lead to an even better place for all to work.

In a Monster study, 40% of recruiters said workers ask about their potential employers' DEI efforts "more than ever," but 11% of employers said DEI programs "are among the first to go when they are forced to cut costs." In 2016, former Twitter CEO (Jack Dorsey) vowed to make his company more inclusive during an interview with CODE2040 founder Laura Weidman Powers. A year later, in 2017, more than 2,400 CEOs signed the CEO Action for Diversity and Inclusion pledge, claiming diversity and inclusion are priorities. Companies doubled down on this commitment following the George Floyd protests in 2020. It appeared DEI was top of mind for many organizations' leaders.

Fast forward to 2023. With the threat of a recession looming like a storm cloud over the economy, some companies, especially in tech, have already started reducing their diversity teams. Twitter's DEI team drops from 30 to two employees, and its ERGS is completely dissolved. On LinkedIn, a former Lyft employee shared that she, along with most of the diversity and inclusion team, was cut. Companies that were all in just two years ago are backing away from their DEI commitments, forcing DEI leaders to pursue new opportunities.

You are burned out. WE are burned out! In DEI, the finish line is always moving forward. You learn quickly that you must be able to play a long game internally, within yourself. Some have said DEI work is half-frustration, half-inspiration. At the end of the day, you must let the frustration go and focus on what you were able to get done.

THE CHIEF DIVERSITY OFFICER ROLE

The simple title of Chief brings a lot of power. For some boards, the role of Chief must be voted on by a majority vote of the board. Let us look at the dilemma of the CDO Role.

You have probably heard the rumor that CDOs tend to leave their roles within two years. The question is how much of that short tenure is because the CDO role is not respected and how much is because individuals like women, women of color, and men of color in those roles have been underestimated. Many women get tired of working in a position that is not respected and/or of bouncing around—so if they have the means, they leave to become a consultant.

While there are great things about working for oneself, in many ways, DEI consultants have even fewer opportunities than in-house CDOs. They are more likely to be asked to speak on panels or contribute their opinions if they work for large, well-known corporations. Often, when that same CDO leaves their role for self-employment, they are no longer sought-after because they need to come with a familiar brand name and logo. I know of several women who worked in high-profile positions for big companies who were uninvited from panel discussions when they left their big employers. This makes it clear that the host of those panels does not care about the expertise of the individual but the associated brand name. As DEI remains a non-negotiable topic across leadership and the workplace, better data comes out about the identities of people in these roles and how that intersects with the expectations of and respect for the role itself. In the meantime, organizations can do something different by making the CDO role a position that is respected. If the rest of the executive team does not appreciate DEI or see its value, if it is not tied to the company's business goals and values, then why have it?

In the closing section of Stacey Gordon's book, *UNBIAS: Addressing Unconscious Bias at Work*, she outlines key indicators that suggest a CDO role will be influential, indicating that it is both valued and respected. These indicators include:

- Reporting directly to the CEO rather than Human Resources.
- Having the authority to implement recommended personnel changes, irrespective of the seniority of the individuals involved.
- Holding individuals accountable to the values and strategy set by the company's leaders.

These indicators, and many more, go a long way toward ensuring that the CDO's role is respected. It is the mandate for all to unlearn these unconscious biases, ensuring that the identities of the individuals in CDO roles are respected, no matter what they are. There are a number of articles circulating that make the case that CDOs are being disproportionately affected by layoffs and that those who remain are primarily White.

Once again, more data is needed to make this case because what we are seeing in the industry makes it such that you cannot fire someone who has already quit. On the other hand, reports already lend support to this idea, as many women and professionals of color are usually the first to be impacted when layoffs happen. If those roles are filled with women and professionals of color, it makes sense that there would be a disproportionate number of DEI positions that are on the chopping block. There continues to be enthusiasm for employee initiatives, along with continued frustration about stagnant progress. Research studies show that the average duration of a chief diversity officer ranges from one to three and a half years, marking CDOs as having the shortest tenure among their C-Suite peers. Many in these roles have left the CDO track altogether. High CDO turnover might have employees wondering if the company truly prioritizes DEI as a business strategy.

A recent report exploring data from the United States also revealed that fewer people are trying to improve DEI even though under-representation, a lack of belonging, and lower attention for those from under-represented groups persist. And these issues are not limited to the US. Research also supports that diversity fatigue is a worldwide problem. Though companies are raising awareness of DEI efforts, they've yet to affect lasting behavioral, cultural, and structural change. Many say improvements are optional, even though little progress has been made, which suggests there is a severe perception gap between what people think diversity means and what progress really looks like.

ALLYSHIP

Being an ally means actively working to promote the well-being and advancement of a group of people who may face systemic discrimination or oppression. Here are some ways to practice allyship:

> Listen and learn: Listen to experiences and concerns and educate yourself about the issues people are facing. Read books and articles written by others outside of the group you identify with. Watching movies and documentaries that highlight diverse stories and attending workshops or events that focus on gender equality is another way to be an ally.
>
> Speak up: When you hear someone make a racist, sexist, or disrespectful comment, speak up and challenge their behavior. Do not be a passive bystander, but instead use your voice to call out bad behavior.
>
> Amplify the voices of others: Use your privilege and platform to amplify diverse voices and support those causes. Share their work on social media, invite them to speak at events or panels, and promote their businesses or projects.
>
> Mentor and sponsor: Offer mentorship and sponsorship opportunities to diverse employees within your workplace or industry. Help marginalized employees develop their skills and advance in their careers by providing guidance, feedback, and support.

We must act and support policies and initiatives that promote gender equality, such as equal pay, paid parental leave, and flexible work arrangements. Vote for candidates who prioritize gender equality and donate to organizations that support women's rights. Remember, being an ally is an ongoing process, and it requires self-reflection, humility, and a willingness to learn and grow.

HR EXPERIENCE

Employment lawyers possess numerous instances and narratives illustrating the economic consequences stemming from inadequate inclusion. While working in human resources, I found myself in a position where I could not directly address the issue. Yet, there were expectations for me to act against the evident lack of inclusion. Why were the Black individuals within the company expected to act? It fell outside the scope of my role and responsibilities to enact change. As an HR team member, I needed more influence or authority to bring about any meaningful transformation.

Understanding this is key to explaining the legitimacy of this concept to companies and stakeholders: to stop putting Black people in these blind alley roles and to stop expecting them to do anything without backup, assistance, and allyship of White people in the company. Often, leaders, including Black leaders, like the fact that they are in these roles and can stifle and stall progress. They seem to enjoy the fact that they can blame the Black person for not having achieved the 'impossible' progress.

The next level of what can be provided as an engine of change is to create real systems in HR policies and practices that manage situations where there are discrimination and/or racial claims. There is an apparent need for actual steps and processes when we have real equity issues. This is where the gap in failed processes is most evident.

What is illusory is that there is no effective practice for intake, resolution, or mediation. There is no owner of the process and no follow-up. So, employees go to the HR Department, and their visits are fruitless, and the issues remain unchanged. There is no accountability. Staff are left flailing in the wind with their skirts and shirts above their heads, vulnerable and cold.

The people at the mic, the whistleblowers, try to help make changes in the process, and they put their jobs at risk. They are pushing the status quo, and they are seen as troublemakers. Bringing issues to the company and forgetting there are dictates like Whistleblower Laws that protect people from retaliation. This is not new, but 'HR 101'—fair and basic employment. The economics of this situation make it so that these 'whistleblower' employees are now stuck. They are forced into a position where they know they should leave their positions for the protection of their mental health—but they will not do it. They do so because they refuse to abandon the other people in the company who have no advocate left for them.

Now, we are left with people who have no advocacy and the continued mechanism of being 'screwed over,' impacting access to opportunities and financial gains. The economic impact of being in roles that pay $200K - $400K to be complicit in the DEI dilemma has a substantial number of repercussions. There is also an economic impact when these DEI practitioners stand up in their professional courage and initiate litigation.

No one wants to talk about this because it is taboo in the workplace. The reality is this is the very way that change is affected. They change because they are sued. They change because they lose money in claims of these lawsuits. They change because they are taken to court—under duress.

Recently, a colleague reached out to me to let me know that they had been asked to lead DEI by their HR Director. Those who agreed to be leaders would receive a $25 stipend for the year. To add insult to injury, they asked her to sign an agreement to confirm that she would lead DEI in her area for the stipend. Please note that I share this with the utmost kindness: the involvement of HR in DEI is often, at best, passive, and at worst, openly disgraceful.

I know, as an HR Professional, how I actively chose not to support marginalized employees due to a combination of being tired, aggravated, and focused on my career. Let us delve more deeply into the role of HR and explore why it may not always be the most suitable division in the organization to lead DEI initiatives.

There are several reasons why some argue that diversity should not be solely managed by the HR department. The first reason is HR's limited perspective. HR may lack the diverse perspectives and experiences needed to effectively address all aspects of diversity. Just because someone is in HR does not mean they understand equity or fairness, for that matter. In fact, I once worked with a top executive in HR who was presented with a potential job candidate—a Native American applicant. For the sake of confidentiality, let us say the person's name was Kele Catwater.

The HR leader admitted that they had concerns about Kele's name. The HR person decided that people might not take the applicant seriously because of their name and that hiring them would be too much of a risk. As the gatekeeper of the culture, it was easy for this leader to decide Kele was not a cultural fit. So, Kele's application remained in limbo. Despite his impressive qualifications, he was a victim of the HR leader's unjust bias. Since HR was the gatekeeper of the overall hiring process, there was no one to challenge the HR leader's decision. Ironically, these discriminating practices were brought to light when the HR team was pressured to attend mandatory DEI training. Other blind spots in the company's HR processes were exposed during these inclusion trainings by an outside consultant.

Another issue for HR involves tokenization concerns. That is, if HR is solely responsible, there's a risk of tokenizing diversity efforts rather than fostering genuine inclusion. And, as mentioned in Kele's story, despite our best intentions, HR staff may inadvertently bring biases into diversity management. Similarly, relying solely on HR can create silos, hindering collaboration with other departments that also play a crucial role in fostering diversity. Partner this with the fact that HR in most organizations may not have the authority or influence required to drive meaningful change across all levels of an organization and usually operate in a consultative role.

Keep in mind that just because employees are in HR does not automatically imply that they are trained on equity issues. HR professionals are not always adequately trained in diversity issues. This lack of training leads to potential mishandling of sensitive matters. In fact, HR may struggle to fully understand and address the diverse cultural nuances within an organization.

Last but certainly not least, I have experienced first-hand employees' skepticism of HR's ability to address diversity effectively, given historical shortcomings or perceived conflicts of interest. This is why it is important to promote successful diversity initiatives through a more collaborative and cross-functional approach involving various departments within an organization.

VIII
POLICY FORCES CHANGE

"If you stick a knife nine inches into my back and pull it out three inches, that is not progress. Even if you pull it all the way out, that is not progress. Progress is healing the wound, and America hasn't even begun to pull out the knife." - Malcolm X

In order to fully comprehend the dilemma, you must look at American policies. Since the inception of this country, there have been policies enacted that impact equity within the workforce. In this section, I will highlight some of the policies that have impacted marginalized groups in America.

Affirmative Action: Affirmative action refers to policies and initiatives that seek to increase representation and opportunities for historically underrepresented groups, such as women, racial and ethnic minorities, and people with disabilities. These policies have been implemented in various sectors, including education and employment, to promote diversity and mitigate historical discrimination.

Civil Rights Act of 1964: This landmark legislation was enacted to end segregation in public places and prohibit discrimination based on race, color, religion, sex, or national origin. The Act aimed to ensure greater equity and access to opportunities for marginalized communities.

Voting Rights Act of 1965: The Voting Rights Act aimed to address racial discrimination in voting practices, especially in the Southern states. It eliminated discriminatory voting practices that had historically disenfranchised minority voters, particularly African Americans.

Fair Housing Act of 1968: This legislation aimed to address housing discrimination based on race, color, national origin, religion, sex, familial status, or disability. It sought to create more equitable access to housing opportunities for marginalized communities.

Affordable Care Act (ACA) - "Obamacare": The ACA aimed to increase access to healthcare for millions of Americans by expanding Medicaid eligibility, providing subsidies for insurance premiums, and prohibiting insurers from denying coverage based on pre-existing conditions. This policy aimed to reduce healthcare disparities and increase equity in healthcare access.

Education Reform: Various policies and initiatives at the federal and state levels have attempted to address educational disparities based on factors such as race, socioeconomic status, and disability. These include efforts to increase funding for underprivileged schools, implement early childhood education programs, and address systemic issues affecting marginalized students.

Criminal Justice Reform: Various efforts have been made to address disparities in the criminal justice system, including sentencing reform, alternatives to incarceration, and initiatives to reduce racial profiling and bias in law enforcement.

LGBTQ+ Rights: Policies and legal changes have sought to promote equity and equality for the LGBTQ+ and Queer community, such as the legalization of same-sex marriage nationwide and the protection against discrimination based on sexual orientation and gender identity in various contexts.

CROWN ACT - The Crown Act, short for "Creating a Respectful and Open World for Natural Hair," holds significant importance in addressing a deeply rooted issue of racial discrimination and promoting equality. This legislation has emerged as a response to the longstanding and unjust practice of penalizing individuals, primarily Black people, for wearing natural hairstyles like braids, afros, twists, and locs in professional and public spaces.

The significance of the Crown Act lies in its potential to dismantle harmful stereotypes and biases surrounding natural hair. For far too long, societal norms and beauty standards have favored Eurocentric hair textures, implicitly suggesting that natural Black hair is unprofessional or unkempt. This has led to instances of systemic discrimination, with individuals facing scrutiny, derogatory comments, or even job loss due to their choice of natural hairstyles. The Crown Act's importance lies in its ability to challenge these discriminatory practices, fostering a more inclusive and respectful environment for people of all backgrounds to express their cultural identity authentically.

By enacting the Crown Act, lawmakers acknowledge the need to confront systemic racism and challenge the status quo. This legislation sends a clear message that no one should be subjected to discrimination based on their hair texture or style. It reinforces the fundamental principle of equality and the right for individuals to express their cultural heritage without fear of repercussions. Moreover, the Crown

Act contributes to a broader conversation about the importance of diverse representation and inclusion, not only in the workplace but also in society.

Beyond its immediate impact, the Crown Act carries symbolic weight as a step toward dismantling deeply ingrained biases. It challenges the historical legacy of discrimination against Black people and recognizes the importance of embracing cultural diversity. The Act's significance extends beyond legislation; it sparks conversations about identity, representation, and the power of embracing one's natural self. As more states and jurisdictions adopt the Crown Act, its impact ripples through institutions, fostering a more accepting society where everyone can confidently wear their "crown" of natural hair, free from prejudice and discrimination.

One common element in the civil rights, equity, and DEI movement is the importance of policy and federal laws to help drive the moment. The Family and Medical Leave Act (FMLA), the Americans with Disabilities Act (ADA), Workers Comp, and other job protection laws continue to provide protections and support for employees experiencing racial discrimination, inequity, and unfairness in the workplace.

FMLA, the ADA, and other medical leave policies collectively offer essential protections for employees who feel discriminated against in the workplace due to various factors, including disabilities and health-related issues. FMLA provides eligible employees with up to 12 weeks of unpaid, job-protected leave per year for specific family or medical reasons. These reasons include the employee's serious health condition, the need to care for a spouse, child, or parent with a serious health condition, or the arrival of a new child through birth, adoption, or foster care. This protection ensures that employees who face discrimination based on their health conditions can take the necessary time off to manage their medical needs without fear of losing their jobs.

The Americans with Disabilities Act (ADA) prohibits discrimination against individuals with disabilities in all areas of public life, including employment. ADA mandates that employers provide reasonable accommodations to qualified employees with disabilities, allowing them to perform their job responsibilities effectively. Suppose an employee believes they are being discriminated against due to their disability. In that case, they can request accommodations that enable them to carry out their work tasks on an equal footing with their colleagues. This protection ensures that individuals with disabilities can participate fully in the workplace without facing unjust treatment.

Medical leave policies, often established by employers, supplement the protections offered by FMLA and ADA. These policies outline how employees can request and take medical leave for health-related issues that might not fall within the specific criteria of FMLA or ADA. Such guidelines ensure that employees facing health challenges are given the time they need to recover or address their medical concerns without the fear of retribution.

Collectively, these legal provisions and policies create a safety net for employees who feel discriminated against due to their health conditions. By offering leave, accommodations, and protections against discrimination, these regulations contribute to a more equitable and inclusive work environment, allowing employees to address their health needs while maintaining their employment status and opportunities.

Think about the impact of these laws. These laws provide employees with the right to take leave to care for themselves or their loved ones without the fear of losing their jobs. They have mandated that employers provide reasonable accommodations for individuals with disabilities, making workplaces more inclusive and equitable. These laws are a testament to the fact that policies can drive societal change.

For example, workers' compensation is more than just financial support for injured employees. It is a commitment to worker safety and well-being. And when we talk about racial discrimination, inequity, and unfairness, we are often addressing invisible wounds—emotional scars that impact an employee's mental health and overall wellness. The fight for fair treatment is not just about finances; it is about creating an environment where all employees can thrive.

There is a need for comprehensive policies that address racial discrimination head-on, including the importance of whistleblower protections, which enable employees to come forward without fearing retaliation. It is important to emphasize the significance of equal pay laws that seek to eradicate gender and racial pay disparities.

In the journey toward a more just and equitable workplace, these laws and policies are our allies. They are the tools we wield to dismantle the barriers that have held marginalized individuals back for far too long. But remember, these laws are only as effective as our efforts to enforce them. It is up to all of us to hold employers accountable, to use the legal framework, to push for change, and to continue the march toward progress.

The Department of Labor (DOL) plays a vital role in protecting the rights of employees who fall into protected classes. The DOL policies are designed to provide a safety net and to ensure appropriate behavior by employees who are prone to bias and discriminatory practices. The DOL stands as a critical guardian of employees' rights, particularly for those who belong to protected classes and face discrimination or bias in the workplace. With its comprehensive policies and proactive approach, the DOL acts as a beacon of guidance, offering a safety net that bolsters the dignity and rights of every individual in the workforce.

The DOL's involvement extends to the enforcement of numerous federal laws aimed at eradicating discrimination and promoting workplace equity. From overseeing the implementation of the FMLA and the Fair Labor Standards Act (FLSA) to upholding the principles of equal pay and occupational safety, the DOL's initiatives address a broad spectrum of employee concerns.

One of the DOL's significant roles is to set standards and regulations that ensure fair treatment of workers. These regulations encompass issues like minimum wage, overtime pay, and safe working conditions, impacting a diverse range of employees across industries. By holding employers accountable to these standards, the DOL contributes to fostering an environment where all employees, regardless of their background or protected class, are treated fairly and with respect. In cases where employees face bias or discriminatory practices, the DOL's policies serve as a deterrent against such behavior. By establishing clear guidelines and consequences for violations, the DOL encourages workplaces to adopt a culture of inclusivity and equal treatment. This not only benefits individual employees but also strengthens the overall health and productivity of the workforce.

In essence, the DOL functions as a cornerstone of protection for employees. Its policies and oversight not only ensure that workers are treated justly, but they also signal a commitment to fostering workplaces that are free from bias and discrimination. As a result, the DOL contributes to shaping a more equitable landscape where all employees can thrive, irrespective of their background, identity, or membership in protected classes.

IX
REAL EQUITY

"Diversity really means becoming complete as human beings – all of us. We learn from each other. If you're missing on that stage, we learn less. We all need to be on that stage." – Juan Felipe Herrera

BIPOC folks should not have to regurgitate their trauma or be "perfect victims" to be worthy of having their humanity recognized. Sadly, many DEI training methods require People of Color to rehash their traumas to educate White people and try to elicit empathy. We need to shift away from focusing on empathy and White egos and towards taking strategic action to address racism. Career advancement for underrepresented groups is a social justice issue. Being promoted at work enables power and influence.

This is an anecdote for unconscious bias. The word equity itself sparks fear and other emotions in specific settings. The pressure to perform and conform in business often leads to elevated levels of stress. Adding to the tension are feelings of loneliness and disconnection.

According to executive search firm Russell Reynolds data, the average CDO tenure is now under two years, compared to more than three years in 2018. Nearly 60% of 2018 CDOs have left their roles, with the majority going on the CDO track for other professional interests. Only 18% of current CDOs have prior experience in the position, down from 26% in 2018. Ask yourself, where have we ever seen statistics like this regarding a function in an organization?

When an organization designates a specific department responsible for DEI, the ownership and accountability for these efforts are shifted away from executive decision-makers. As a result, DEI becomes seen as a compartmentalized issue handled by a select group of individuals (usually short-staffed and facing burn-out) rather than an embedded value upheld by leadership and all employees. This leads to a workplace mentality where other departments only address DEI when faced with related problems instead of proactively working towards creating an inclusive environment.

To facilitate substantial organizational change, alter perspectives, and integrate DEI values into the structure, here are practical steps to effectively approach DEI and instill change:

> Conduct Comprehensive DEI Audits: Hire external consultants to conduct thorough audits identifying gaps in the organization's diversity and inclusion efforts. These audits should extend beyond representation numbers and delve into policies, practices, and organizational culture. Only conduct an exhaustive audit if you have done something with previously collected relevant data.

Increase Education and Awareness: DEI is a change process. Promote DEI Organizational change education and training for leaders first, then for all employees. This education should teach strategies for effective transformation. Do not conduct polarizing training that focuses on comparatives between privilege and marginalization.

Establish Accountability Measures: Implement tangible metrics and hold all employees accountable for meeting DEI goals. Tie DEI performance to executive and management evaluations to reinforce its importance across all levels. Do not implement measurements that you do not hold boards and executives to; people see these disingenuous actions.

Utilize the Expertise of DEI Professionals: Leverage the expertise of executives who have previously held DEI roles. Many become independent consultants who can offer valuable guidance and insight on implementing effective DEI strategies. Only hire DEI consultants and experts after researching the field and understanding their work.

Leadership as Champions of Change: Ensure that executive leaders champion and actively participate in DEI initiatives. Their commitment strongly signals the organization's values, encouraging others to embrace and support change. Do not keep executives that work against equity; your leadership gaps will be exposed.

The fading out of DEI departments is a natural evolution of organizational approaches towards genuine equity and inclusion. DEI specialists understand the importance of moving beyond performative gestures and adopting comprehensive strategies that involve the entire organization. By embedding DEI values into the company's fabric, employing external expertise, and holding leadership accountable, organizations can pave the way for a more inclusive and equitable future.

Change is a gradual process, and building an inclusive environment requires commitment from all levels of the organization. Let us move away from short-lived, departmental efforts and focus on creating a workplace where diversity, equity, and inclusion thrive as shared values upheld by all.

X
RECRUITING FOR INCLUSION

"I've traveled around the world, and what's so revealing is that, despite the differences in culture, politics, language, and how people dress, there is a universal feeling that we all want the same thing. We deeply want to be respected and appreciated for our differences."
– Howard Schultz

Recruiting for diversity. This is a hot topic! In this section, I will present information that I found that could have been beneficial when I first started out. When recruiting for diversity using ratios, there are a few key steps to consider.

Assess your current workforce: Start by examining the demographics of your current employees to identify areas where diversity could be improved. Determine the ideal ratios or representation goals you want to achieve.

Define inclusive job descriptions: Craft job descriptions that use inclusive language and focus on skills and qualifications rather than specific backgrounds or demographics. This helps attract a diverse pool of candidates.

Broaden recruitment channels: Expand your recruitment efforts beyond traditional channels to reach a wider audience. Consider posting job openings on specialized job boards, attending career fairs at diverse colleges and universities, partnering with various professional organizations, and utilizing social media platforms.

Build diverse interview panels: Ensure that the interview panels are diverse and representative of different backgrounds and perspectives. This helps create an inclusive and unbiased interview process.

Implement blind screening: Remove identifying information such as names, genders, or ages from resumes during the initial screening process. This reduces potential biases and allows for a more objective evaluation of candidates' qualifications.

Provide diversity and inclusion training: Train hiring managers and interviewers on unconscious biases, diversity, and inclusion best practices. This helps them make fair and objective decisions during the selection process.

Establish diversity-focused partnerships: Collaborate with organizations and institutions that promote diversity and inclusion. This can include partnerships with diverse professional associations, community groups, or diversity-focused recruitment agencies.

Measure and track progress: Continuously monitor and evaluate the effectiveness of your diversity recruitment efforts. Collect data on the diversity of applicants, interviewees, and hires to assess if you are meeting your desired ratios or representation goal.

Remember that diversity is not just about meeting numerical ratios; it is about creating an inclusive culture where individuals from all backgrounds feel welcome and valued.

The 60 to 1 RECRUITMENT RATIO

The "60 to 1" recruitment method refers to a strategy where an employer aims to review 60 candidates from underrepresented groups for every hire. This approach is commonly associated with DEI efforts in the workplace. The goal is to increase diversity by actively seeking out and considering a larger pool of candidates from traditionally marginalized or underrepresented backgrounds. By implementing the 60 to 1 ratio, organizations strive to address systemic biases and promote equitable opportunities for individuals who may have been historically overlooked in the hiring process.

The most effective DEI recruiting method varies depending on the organization and its specific goals. The following are some commonly utilized strategies.

Diverse job postings: Using inclusive language and reaching out to diverse networks to attract a broader range of candidates.

Targeted outreach: Proactively reaching out to under-represented communities and organizations to build relationships and increase visibility.

Partnerships and sponsorships: Collaborating with diverse professional associations, universities, and community organizations to access diverse talent pools.

Employee referrals: Encouraging current employees to refer qualified candidates from diverse backgrounds.

Blind screening: Implementing blind recruitment practices to minimize bias by removing identifiable information from resumes during the initial screening process.

Structured interviews: Using standardized interview questions and evaluation criteria to ensure fairness and consistency.

Unconscious bias training: Providing training to recruiters and hiring managers to raise awareness and mitigate biases during the selection process.

Employer branding: Demonstrating a commitment to DEI through transparent communication of inclusive practices, employee testimonials, and diversity initiatives.

Internship and mentorship programs: Establishing programs to attract diverse talent at an early stage and provide support and development opportunities.

Data tracking and analysis: Regularly measure and analyze recruitment metrics to identify areas of improvement and assess the impact of DEI initiatives.

Remember, the most effective approach depends on the specific context and goals of the organization, so it is essential to continuously evaluate and adapt strategies for better results. Most importantly, if you aim to increase diversity in your hires, it is crucial to conduct interviews with a broader range of candidates.

FAIR CHANCE HIRING

Fact: Efforts to reduce discrimination against individuals with criminal records have not effectively benefited People of Color. The process of criminalization operates within the intersections of race, class, and gender, resulting in uniform impacts on specific individuals. The stigma associated with criminal records reinforces prevailing assumptions about criminal behavior, contributing to the demand for and widespread accessibility of background checks.

While some business owners currently adopt a pragmatic and non-judgmental approach to criminal records, challenges arise in a political economy characterized by regulation, competition, and litigation. Legislation like "Ban the Box" aims to provide a fair chance by prohibiting inquiries about criminal records until a verbal job offer is made, marking a shift in the system. However, awareness among employers about such policies is crucial.

To address equity and inclusion, there is a call for more flexible hiring and firing practices, emphasizing intimate hiring processes, and understanding candidates' search for meaning and purpose in their work. This approach challenges the conventional focus on potential harm and calls for a reconsideration of the presumed necessity of employment background checks.

Hiring managers can actively support fair chance hiring by reframing criminal records as examples of poor choices rather than proof of bad character or guilt. It is essential to resist narratives that rely on personal responsibility or racial uplift as persuasive tools. True empowerment involves releasing Black and BIPOC populations from systems that hold them back and shifting towards economic power as a means of creating an inclusive and equitable society.

CHANGE REQUIRES MEASUREMENTS

There is not a single "best" formula to measure DEI in an organization, as it can vary based on the organization's specific goals and context. However, below are some commonly used metrics and approaches.

> Representation Metrics: Measure the diversity of your workforce across various dimensions, such as gender, race, ethnicity, age, and other protected characteristics. This can be done through headcount ratios, employee surveys, or demographic data analysis.
>
> Employee Engagement Surveys: Include questions related explicitly to DEI to gauge employees' perceptions of inclusion and equity within the organization. This helps identify areas of improvement and track progress over time.
>
> Turnover and Retention Rates: Assess if there are any disparities in turnover rates across different demographic groups. Higher turnover among underrepresented groups may indicate underlying DEI issues.
>
> Pay Equity Analysis: Conduct an analysis to identify and address any gender or racial pay gaps within the organization. This helps ensure fair compensation practices.

Leadership Representation: Evaluate the diversity of leadership positions within the organization. This can be done by tracking the representation of underrepresented groups in managerial or executive roles.

Employee Resource Groups Participation: Measure the participation and engagement levels of employees in ERGs or affinity groups focused on diversity and inclusion. This reflects employees' interest and involvement in DEI efforts.

Supplier Diversity: Assess the diversity of your organization's suppliers and contractors to promote inclusivity throughout the supply chain.

Remember, these metrics should be used in conjunction with qualitative insights and feedback from employees to gain a comprehensive understanding of an organization's DEI efforts and progress.

RUN, DON'T WALK

A few years ago, I eagerly accepted the role of Regional HR Manager at a prestigious entertainment company, prompting my family to relocate from the East Coast to the West Coast for a six-figure salary – a first for me despite my extensive experience and master's in business. As one of the first in my family to graduate from college and earn a master's degree, this move marked a significant achievement. Managing HR for over 3,000 people in the western region felt like a major accomplishment.

Upon starting the role, I learned that a mass layoff affecting many Black, Brown, and Tan seasonal workers was imminent. Despite feeling like a spy and a fraud, I was tasked with coordinating the exit without input and encouraged to gain trust and assess individuals for potential retention. I felt used and powerless, but my commitment to integrity led me to handle the situation with empathy. Drawing on experience, I provided resources and ensured a dignified exit for those affected.

In the subsequent years, my caring reputation led employees to approach me for support in diversity initiatives. Recognizing the absence of such programs in the large company, I committed to working behind the scenes to make diversity a priority. After two years, the CEO asked me to spearhead a diversity initiative. While the initial job description was vague, I eventually secured the title of VP of Diversity, accompanied by a 10% salary increase. The role, however, came with a demotion to a cubicle and the challenging task of leading DEI in an organization not fully ready for change. Despite recognizing the personal cost to my career and well-being, it was a sacrifice worth making to create positive change.

Here are signs that you need to run and not walk from a request to lead DEI within an organization or from the organization entirely. The company asks you to lead the initiative; it is new and has no direction. For example, you may encounter challenges if the leaders of the organization lack clarity on aspects such as the job title, salary, the purpose behind creating the role, who your reporting manager will be, and so on. You know you are lacking leadership, management, business, or human resources experience. Trust me, it is a setup. Especially if you just happen to be the only Black person in the company or department. Be honest with yourself and make sure you get the training needed.

They have been working on the same strategies for 5 – 10 years (basing this on the ability to make real change using a 5-year plan), and some of the basic DEI activities such as ERGs, diverse imaging, and DEI training are not in place. They need a budget and want to avoid creating a budget to pay you or your team for the effort.

INCLUSION DELUSION

Toni Lowe, Global Diversity, Equity, and Inclusion Executive, identifies the first delusion as isolating progress to one demographic and neglecting the impact of stagnation on other marginalized groups. There will always be experiences in the workplace that vary, but being micro-focused on one identity as a pillar of progress can create further marginalization.

According to Lowe, delusion is believing that inclusion means everyone must be happy and satisfied or that inclusion cures all ills. The delusion that inclusion equals happiness leads to an opposite outcome. A pseudo-community where people who have counter opinions and/or marginalized experiences have no place in your organization if they do not deem it as consistently positive. Groups trapped in this delusion hold up a false kind of status difference that values people who act happy more than people who have feedback, which may be seen as polarizing. This delusion creates a disconnect in who your organization says it is versus how it behaves.

XI
THE ROAD TO INCLUSION

"Inclusion is a powerful idea that can be achieved by using our imaginations." – Dr. Thelá Thatch

Embarking on the path to inclusion demands confronting various obstacles head-on. Progress faces a significant hurdle when it is limited to a single demographic, overlooking the far-reaching consequences of stagnation on other marginalized groups. While workplace experiences differ, hyper-focusing on a single identity as the epitome of progress can exacerbate marginalization. The delusion that inclusion guarantees universal happiness is misleading; in reality, it often results in the opposite. This misguided belief fosters a pseudo-community where dissenting opinions or marginalized experiences are unwelcome unless consistently positive, perpetuating a false hierarchy that values outward happiness over constructive feedback. Consequently, this delusion creates a glaring disparity between an organization's professed identity and its actual behavior.

Recognizing this, I have come to understand that genuine inclusion requires a pragmatic plan and strategy. In my experience, employing clear and concise frameworks has proven effective in mitigating confusion and overall frustration surrounding justice, equity, and diversity efforts, ultimately fostering a state of inclusion. I've crafted three frameworks tailored to different stages of your journey.

The first framework, the 7 A's, initiates conversations within your organizations and communities. Next, I introduce the 7 D's, designed to deliberately challenge the status quo through pointed questions and exercises, aiming to dismantle barriers hindering the achievement of the 7 A's.

The last framework, the 7 R's, focuses on the most crucial aspect of this journey – you. Research has proven that by prioritizing your rest, renewal, and overall well-being, you can effectively sustain the ongoing quest for inclusion and equity. Let's delve into these frameworks together.

THE 7A, 7D & 7R FRAMEWORKS

The 7 As

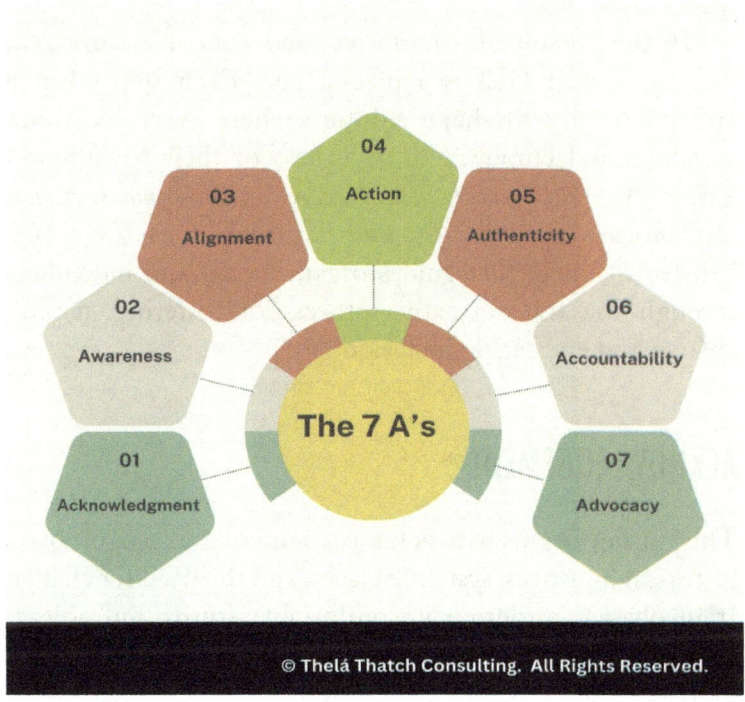

An additional framework I have built further upon involves the 7 As. I refer to this as the 7 As framework. In her book *Unbiased*, Stacey Gordon describes the 4 As of Awareness, Alignment, Action, and Advocacy. As I used this model in my work, I began to discover the opportunity to build on Stacey's framework to provide additional instruction to leaders.

As I used this model in my work, I began to discover the opportunity to build on Stacey's framework to provide additional instruction to leaders.

Action, and Advocacy. As I used this model in my work, I began to discover the need to provide additional instruction to leaders. For example, it became clear that before we could reach awareness, we needed to acknowledge that there was no awareness.

In the pursuit of a more just and equitable world, the journey toward DEI is a pivotal one. Each step taken is an opportunity to shape a future where every individual is valued and empowered, regardless of their background. The 7 As—*Acknowledgment, Awareness, Alignment, Action, Authenticity, Accountability, and Advocacy*—form a comprehensive roadmap that guides organizations and individuals through the transformative process of fostering genuine change and embracing inclusion.

ACKNOWLEDGEMENT

The journey begins with acknowledgment—a recognition of historical injustices, systemic biases, and the need for change. It involves confronting uncomfortable truths and accepting that inequalities exist. By acknowledging these realities, individuals and institutions set the stage for a journey rooted in authenticity and growth.

AWARENESS

Awareness is the lens through which we see the world. Developing awareness means actively seeking to understand the experiences and challenges faced by different communities. It involves actively listening, learning from lived experiences, and embracing diverse viewpoints. Increased awareness fosters empathy and a deeper connection with the realities of marginalized groups.

ALIGNMENT

Incorporating diversity and inclusion into an organization's values and culture requires alignment—a collective commitment to creating an environment where all voices are heard and respected. Alignment ensures that DEI efforts are not isolated initiatives but integral components of an organization's mission and vision.

ACTION

Action is the catalyst for change. Action turns intentions into impact. Tangible steps, both big and small, are needed to effect meaningful change. These actions include diversifying leadership, establishing inclusive policies, and creating safe spaces for marginalized voices. The power of action lies in its ability to transform awareness and intentions into concrete outcomes.

AUTHENTICITY

Authenticity is key to creating a genuinely inclusive environment. Embracing identity and encouraging individuals to bring their whole selves to the table fosters a sense of belonging. Authenticity acknowledges the intersectionality of identities and celebrates the uniqueness of each individual's lived experiences.

ACCOUNTABILITY

Holding oneself and others accountable is essential to sustaining progress. Accountability involves recognizing missteps, learning from them, and actively working to rectify any harm caused. It also demands acknowledging the results of DEI efforts and being transparent about ongoing initiatives.

ADVOCACY

Advocacy transcends personal or organizational boundaries. It entails leveraging one's privilege and influence to uplift and amplify the voices of marginalized communities. Advocates actively challenge discriminatory practices, promote inclusivity, and work toward dismantling systemic barriers.

The 7 As represent a comprehensive approach to diversity, equity, and inclusion. Each "A" contributes to the development of a multifaceted strategy that acknowledges the past, embraces the present, and shapes the future. By moving through these stages with intention and sincerity, individuals and organizations can contribute to a world where diversity is celebrated, equity is realized, and inclusion is the norm. The journey toward a more just and inclusive society is ongoing, and the 7 As provides a roadmap for every step of the way.

The 7 Ds BLUEPRINT

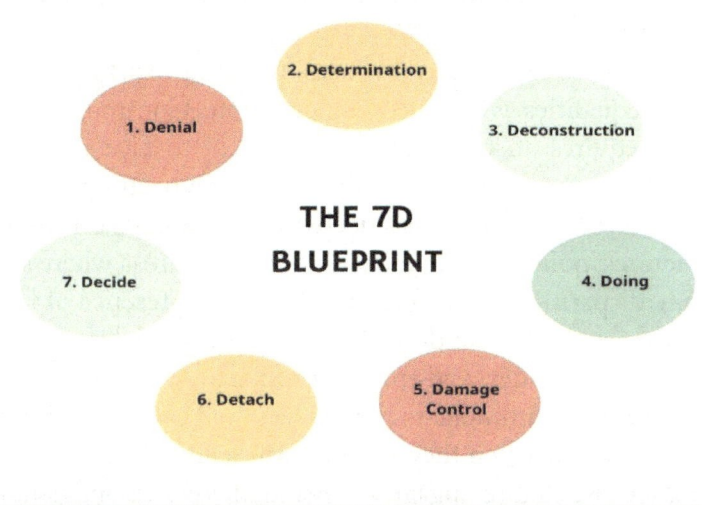

Establishing a truly inclusive and equitable organization requires a strategic methodology that tackles challenges and opportunities inherent at every phase of transformation. The progression from denial to decision involves crucial measures pivotal to substantial change. I have formulated a blueprint for organizational transformation aptly named the 7 D Blueprint. This blueprint serves as a guide for organizations to cultivate a culture entrenched in DEI. Now, let us delve into the components that comprise this blueprint.

DENIAL

The journey from denial to awareness is a critical phase in the pursuit of DEI within any organization. It is a transformative process that involves shedding the protective layers of denial and embracing the uncomfortable truths that lie beneath the surface. This phase signifies a profound shift in perspective, heralding a commitment to address biases and inequalities head-on.

We must face reality by acknowledging existing biases and inequalities within the organization. Confronting the truth requires an unwavering willingness to face the reality of biases and inequalities that may have been ignored or downplayed. This involves a deep dive into the organization's structures, policies, and practices to identify areas where systemic disparities exist. Acknowledging the presence of bias, whether explicit or subtle, is the first step toward dismantling it. It requires leaders and employees alike to recognize that no organization is immune to these issues, and genuine progress can only occur when they are honestly acknowledged.

It is essential to engage in open dialogues to understand the experiences of marginalized groups. Listening becomes a powerful tool in the journey toward awareness. Opening up spaces for marginalized voices to share their experiences provides invaluable insights into the lived realities of those who have been adversely affected by bias and inequality. Honest conversations, guided by empathy and active listening, allow employees to understand the challenges faced by their colleagues. This process builds bridges of understanding and compassion, laying the foundation for a more inclusive culture. Investing in DEI training is necessary to raise awareness among employees but should be a part of a larger strategy. Education is a cornerstone of transformation.

Organizations committed to moving from denial to awareness invest in DEI training and workshops that equip their workforce with the knowledge and skills needed to recognize and address bias. These initiatives offer a structured approach to fostering awareness, enabling employees to grasp the intricacies of systemic inequalities, unconscious bias, and the far-reaching impact of microaggressions. Education empowers individuals to challenge their assumptions and actively contribute to the creation of a more equitable environment. Confronting the truth during this phase requires courage, vulnerability, and a collective commitment to change. It is a pivotal moment that paves the way for subsequent stages of the DEI journey, including accountability, action, and transformation. By acknowledging biases, listening to marginalized voices, and investing in education, organizations lay the groundwork for a culture that is both inclusive and equitable. This type of culture acknowledges its flaws and takes decisive steps toward a better future.

DETERMINATION

The phase of determination marks a critical juncture in the journey toward fostering DEI within an organization. It is a phase characterized by strategic intention, where the organization sets its sights on a more equitable and inclusive future. This phase encapsulates the proactive steps taken to lay a strong foundation for DEI initiatives that will catalyze lasting change.

At the heart of determination lies the creation of a well-defined DEI vision and mission statement. This foundational step encapsulates the organization's aspirations for a more inclusive future and communicates its commitment to all stakeholders. A clear and compelling DEI vision articulates the organization's ultimate goal—a workplace where diversity is celebrated, equity is upheld, and inclusion is embedded in every facet of operations. This vision not only guides the organization's actions but also resonates with employees, fostering a sense of purpose and shared direction.

Leadership commitment is a linchpin in the determination phase.

For DEI initiatives to flourish, top leadership must actively endorse and champion them. Their visible commitment sets the tone for the entire organization, signaling that DEI is not just a buzzword but a strategic imperative. When leaders demonstrate a genuine dedication to change, it filters down to all levels, inspiring employees to participate wholeheartedly. Leadership's advocacy also underscores that DEI initiatives are not isolated efforts but integral to the organization's success.

Determination requires tangible investments, both in terms of finances and human capital. Allocating adequate resources demonstrates the organization's seriousness about translating its DEI vision into reality. Financial support is essential for implementing comprehensive training programs, supporting employee resource groups, and facilitating initiatives that promote equity and inclusion. Equally important is the allocation of human resources—assigning dedicated personnel to oversee and drive DEI initiatives ensures that progress is systematic and sustainable. The determination phase is marked by an unwavering commitment to effect change. It involves formulating a clear vision, rallying leadership support, and backing up intentions with the necessary resources. This phase creates a roadmap for subsequent stages, guiding the organization towards impactful actions that will disrupt the status quo and shape a more inclusive future. By setting a resolute course and marshaling the forces of change, organizations embrace their role as architects of a transformed workplace—one that thrives on diversity, champions equity, and welcomes every individual's voice and contribution.

DECONSTRUCTION

The phase of deconstruction to action represents the pivotal moment where intention transforms into tangible change. It is a stage where the organization dismantles the barriers that have long hindered DEI efforts and proactively engages in the reconstruction of a more just and equitable workplace. This phase marks a commitment to not just acknowledge existing inequalities but to undertake meaningful steps towards rectifying them.

Central to the deconstruction phase is a thorough review of existing organizational policies and practices. It is a reckoning with the structures that may inadvertently perpetuate bias and inequality. Scrutinizing policies through a DEI lens exposes areas where systemic barriers might be embedded. It is a courageous act of holding up a mirror to the organization's practices, acknowledging shortcomings, and committing to realign them with the principles of equity and inclusion.

The deconstruction phase entails a comprehensive evaluation of the organization's structural framework. It is an acknowledgment that many barriers to inclusion are deeply ingrained in organizational systems. Meaningful change requires more than surface-level adjustments; it necessitates structural transformation. This might involve reimagining reporting structures, promoting transparency in decision-making, and ensuring that promotions and opportunities are accessible to all, regardless of background.

One of the cornerstones of this phase is overhauling recruitment practices to attract diverse talent. This goes beyond the conventional notion of diversity and extends to fostering inclusivity at all levels of the organization. It involves revisiting job descriptions, ensuring they are unbiased and appealing to a wide range of candidates. Moreover, it encompasses diversifying recruitment channels and expanding outreach to communities that have historically been underrepresented.

The deconstruction to action phase is a declaration of intent to turn rhetoric into reality. It is a promise to do the heavy lifting required to break down the structural impediments that hinder diversity and equality. By scrutinizing policies, making structural changes, and reimagining recruitment practices, organizations pave the way for substantive progress. This phase is a testament to the organization's commitment to rolling up its sleeves and actively dismantling the obstacles that have long obstructed the path to a more inclusive future.

DOING

The doing phase marks a significant shift from intention to action, embodying the commitment of an organization to concretely implement diversity, equity, and inclusion (DEI) measures. It is a stage where words are translated into deeds, and comprehensive strategies are put in motion to create a workplace that truly reflects the principles of equity and inclusivity.

Central to the doing phase is the deliberate pursuit of diverse representation. This encompasses all facets of the organization, from leadership positions to operational teams and decision-making bodies. It is a recognition that a diverse range of perspectives contributes to more well-rounded decision-making and innovative problem-solving. The journey involves identifying and nurturing talent from underrepresented backgrounds, and breaking down barriers that have historically hindered their advancement.

The doing phase also underscores the importance of ensuring equity in access to benefits, professional growth, and advancement opportunities. Equalizing benefits removes disparities that may exist due to implicit biases, providing a level playing field for all employees. This phase involves creating robust mentorship and sponsorship programs that champion the growth of underrepresented individuals and provide them with the support they need to thrive within the organization.

Inclusivity extends to communication practices. Organizations in the doing phase prioritize creating a communication environment that is respectful and accessible to all. This entails developing strategies for effective communication that consider diverse learning styles, cultural nuances, and varying backgrounds. It also involves facilitating open dialogues that allow employees to share their experiences and perspectives without fear of retribution, fostering a culture of openness and understanding.

The doing phase is characterized by tangible actions that resonate across the organization. It is a stage where diversity and inclusion cease to be mere buzzwords and instead become woven into the fabric of everyday operations. By increasing diverse representation, ensuring equitable benefits, and fostering inclusive communication, organizations demonstrate their commitment to a workplace that celebrates individuality, values fairness, and creates opportunities for all to flourish. This phase lays the foundation for a transformed organizational culture that not only speaks of equity but lives it out in every aspect of its existence.

DAMAGE CONTROL

The damage control phase embodies the organization's commitment to addressing and mitigating any challenges or setbacks that arise during the journey toward DEI. It is a stage that acknowledges that progress is not always linear and that obstacles are inevitable. Instead of allowing these challenges to derail the DEI efforts, organizations in this phase take proactive measures to navigate and rectify issues.

In this phase, organizations adopt a proactive stance by anticipating potential resistance to DEI initiatives and addressing it promptly. This involves identifying pockets of resistance, understanding their underlying causes, and developing strategies to counteract them. Whether it is skepticism from certain employees or pushback from existing structures, a proactive response ensures that concerns are acknowledged and addressed transparently.

Central to damage control is the establishment of a robust feedback mechanism. Organizations that excel in navigating challenges create a safe and confidential channel for employees to express concerns or share their experiences. This allows employees to voice their thoughts without fear of retribution, providing valuable insights into areas that may require improvement. By actively listening to employee feedback, organizations can identify pain points, course-correct, and demonstrate their commitment to continuous improvement.

The damage control phase is closely tied to cultivating a learning culture. It is important to encourage learning from mistakes and evolving in response to challenges. Organizations recognize that setbacks are opportunities for growth and refinement. Instead of dwelling on mistakes, they promote a mindset of learning and evolution. Mistakes are seen as stepping stones to progress, enabling the organization to refine its approach, correct course, and strengthen its DEI initiatives. This culture of continuous learning instills resilience and adaptability in the face of challenges.

The damage control phase is a testament to an organization's resilience and commitment to its DEI journey. It signifies an unwavering dedication to addressing challenges head-on, learning from setbacks, and demonstrating the agility needed to maintain forward momentum. By taking proactive steps, establishing feedback mechanisms, and fostering a learning culture, organizations not only weather challenges but emerge stronger, more responsive, and more determined to create a workplace that embodies the principles of diversity, equity, and inclusion.

DETACH

Disowning prejudices and biases is a profound commitment to introspection, growth, and fostering a more inclusive worldview. It entails a conscious effort to recognize and relinquish ingrained stereotypes, preconceived notions, and unfair judgments that may influence our thoughts and actions. To disown prejudices is to embark on a journey of self-awareness, acknowledging the existence of biases and actively seeking to dismantle them. It requires individuals to question their assumptions, challenge societal norms, and cultivate empathy for perspectives different from their own. This transformative process involves embracing diversity, promoting open-mindedness, and fostering a genuine appreciation for the richness that comes from acknowledging the unique qualities of every individual. Disowning prejudices is not just about eradicating negative attitudes; it is a commitment to creating a space where everyone is seen, heard, and valued for their authentic selves. This commitment helps to contribute to a more just and harmonious society.

DECIDE

Deciding to commit to change involves strategic planning and developing a DEI strategy that aligns with organizational goals. Metrics and measurement define key performance indicators to track progress. The journey from denial to decision is a transformative process that requires commitment, resilience, and a willingness to adapt.

This blueprint provides a comprehensive roadmap for organizations to follow, acknowledging that change is not linear and requires ongoing effort. By navigating the 7 Ds with intention and determination, organizations can create a more inclusive, equitable, and thriving environment. This brings me to one of my final points regarding Black women. People of Color and those good doers struggling to find their place in DEI. For you, I have created the 7 Rs Blueprint.

THE 7R BLUEPRINT

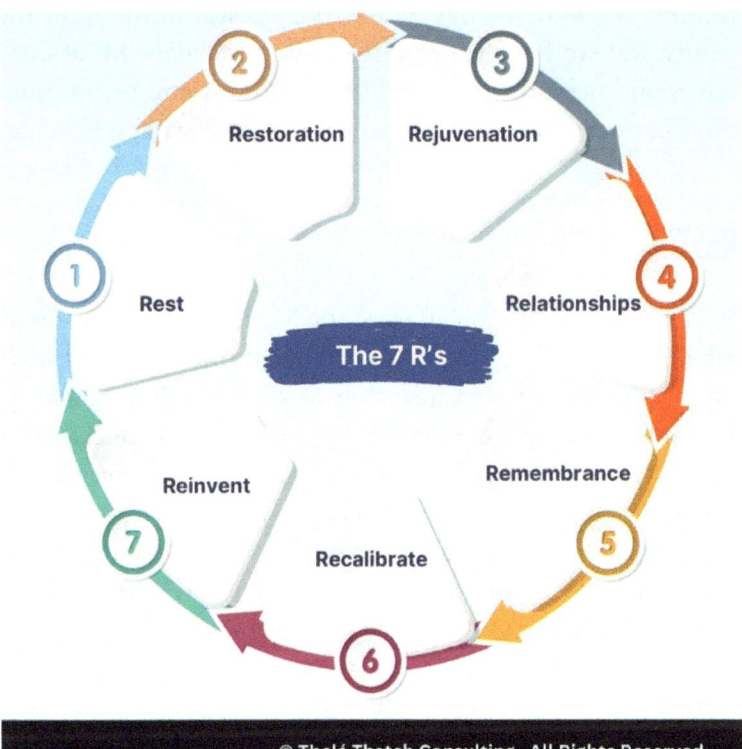

I was at the spa, and being the researcher that I am, I counted the number of Black women who came to the spa. 1-2-3-4- then 5 women by the end of my time. I could say Black women at the spa outnumbered the number of White women and others.

I could not help but think that White people were feeling that the takeover had begun. Well, that was a different type of takeover that needed to continue. A takeover of our mental wellness, of our sistahood of caring for our physical, mental, and spiritual wellness. Yeeeesss! I am excited to see Black women and men taking their health seriously. In fact, I have added massages into my weekly Sunday Sabbath routine. So, as we recognize that we are still in the fight for equity and we have yet to arrive, we must take care of ourselves and fight the good fight through rest and restoration. So, whatever shall we do? Practice the 7Rs is what we can do.

REST

Rest is not merely a break from the battle; it can be an act of rebellion itself. In a world that often glorifies constant hustle, resting becomes an assertion of your worth and agency. It is an opportunity to reject the societal pressure of ceaseless productivity and to fight against the notion that our value is solely defined by what we achieve. By resting, you reclaim your right to mental and physical well-being, reminding the world that your existence is valuable, with or without relentless activity. Rest is a form of resistance, a defiant stand against a culture that seeks to exploit our energy for profit. It is a rebellion against the cycle of burnout that often accompanies the fight for justice.

RESTORATION

Rest is the catalyst for restoration. In the midst of battles, whether personal or societal, we expend vast amounts of emotional and mental energy. Rest offers the opportunity to replenish and restore these precious resources. It is akin to charging a battery. As you rest, you are refueling your capacity to engage with the challenges that lie ahead. It is not a sign of weakness; instead, it is an acknowledgment of your humanity. Just as nature requires seasons of rest to flourish anew, so do individuals require restoration to continue their journey of advocacy and change.

REJUVENATION

Rest breeds rejuvenation. It is the elixir that revives enthusiasm and reignites passion. The process of fighting for justice can be exhausting, and the fire of purpose can dwindle under the weight of adversity. Taking a step back to rest allows you to return with a renewed spirit, ready to face the world with energy and vitality. Rejuvenation is the spark that rekindles your drive and empowers you to continue fighting for what you believe in with even greater fervor.

RELATIONSHIPS

Rest is an opportunity to nurture relationships. Often, in the fervor of a battle, personal connections can take a backseat. Rest gives you the chance to reconnect with loved ones, fostering a sense of belonging and support. Relationships are vital for sustenance; they provide emotional strength and a reminder that you are not alone in your pursuit of justice. Rest offers the space to share stories, exchange experiences, and find solace in the presence of those who understand your journey.

REMEMBRANCE

Rest can be a time for remembrance, a moment to honor those who came before you. Just as we remember the sacrifices and struggles of our ancestors, rest serves as an act of respect for their legacy. It is a way of carrying forward their spirit of resilience and using their time wisely, mindful of the progress they fought so hard to achieve.

RECALIBRATE

Rest is also an opportunity to recalibrate. It is a chance to assess your goals, values, and methods. Stepping back allows you to gain a fresh perspective on your path and to adjust your course if necessary. Recalibration is an acknowledgment that growth requires periodic assessment and realignment. Rest allows you to recalibrate by providing essential time for physical, mental, and emotional recovery. When you rest, your body has the opportunity to repair and regenerate, promoting physical well-being. Additionally, mental fatigue can be alleviated through rest, allowing your mind to process information more effectively and maintain cognitive function.

Emotionally, rest offers a chance to decompress and manage stress, enhancing overall emotional resilience. Taking breaks and allowing yourself to rest can also contribute to better decision-making and problem-solving, as it gives your mind the space it needs to approach challenges with a refreshed perspective.

Personally, I have committed to taking one day a week that I call my Sabbath day to keep my laptop closed. The result for me has been more creativity, clearer thoughts, and actual joy around the work that I get to do.

REINVENT

When we reinvent ourselves, we use everything we have to start again and regroup as many times as needed; give yourself permission to do the 7 Rs as many times as needed; rest can be the space where reinvention is born. It is a clean slate upon which you can redesign your approach. Just as the phoenix rises from its own ashes, rest allows you to shed the old and welcome the new. The journey of fighting for justice is not linear; it is marked by setbacks and challenges. Rest grants you permission to restart, regroup, and reinvent yourself as many times as necessary. It is a reminder that transformation is a constant process and that growth is a continuous cycle of rest, revival, and reinvention.

Let us look at a real-life scenario that illustrates this issue faced by many DEI practitioners. The allure of prestigious positions, coupled with substantial compensation, often leads us to overlook the potential pitfalls and deny our quest for the 7 R's. At worst, we even become unwittingly ensnared in the pursuit of change, slipping into the role of the Black Female Overseer. This figurehead masks deeper systemic inequities and exhausts us even further.

In the final stages of crafting this book, I received an unexpected call—an enticing job opportunity from a renowned entertainment giant, a company symbolizing dreams and happiness. The offer was tempting, inviting me to become a trailblazing leader responsible for championing equity for a workforce of over 45,000. Despite its undeniable allure, I found myself grappling with a critical choice, and here, I share why this was not the ideal role for me.

At first glance, the prospect seemed promising with a substantial salary ranging from $300,000 to $400,000, a team of seventeen, and a role reporting to the CHRO, promising a formidable platform to address equity issues. However, beneath the surface, the dream job began to reveal cracks that could not be ignored.

The organization, despite its century-long legacy, had already proven through media reports and my network that they were faltering in DEI initiatives. The organization had very public issues in executing a robust strategy for integrating equity into its core. The offer coincided with the company's unsettling decision to dismantle equity programs in certain states. The most concerning element was the uncertain assurance that I would be able to shield my mental health from the relentless pressures that often accompany such high-stakes positions. It felt like déjà vu, prompting the question: Was this an opportunity for positive change, or an unwitting descent into a role that would sacrifice my well-being for professional advancement? Despite the initial disbelief at turning down a dream job and more money, I knew that not all that glitter was gold. I walked away whole, confident, and proud of myself for resisting the pressure to accept an offer that could potentially compromise my mental well-being for the sake of professional gain.

As we navigate these critical junctures, it is imperative to arm ourselves with self-preservation skills and steadfast self-care practices. DEI practitioners, your mission to instigate change is crucial, but your well-being is paramount. Embrace radical self-care, prioritize rest, and permit rejuvenation to bolster your resilience. The path to organizational transformation is a persistent journey, and to guarantee its endurance, we must first safeguard our essence.

To those, especially Black women, and People of Color, grappling to find their footing in the realm of DEI, my counsel is straightforward: protect yourself. It is a call to prioritize your mental and emotional well-being more than anything else. Actual change begins within, and only by preserving our vitality can we extend our impact beyond, creating ripples of transformation that endure.

PROTECT YOURSELF

Protecting yourself is an essential mantra in the realm of navigating workplaces. Investigate the organizations you join before you join. Look at the annual report, look at the level of diversity at the top, and look at Glassdoor and other reviews. Before joining any organization, it is imperative to conduct a thorough investigation. You will want to dive into the annual reports, scrutinize the composition of leadership for signs of diversity and inclusion, and delve into platforms like Glassdoor for honest employee reviews.

Next, practice exercising your voice. Alongside this vigilant assessment, empowering yourself through the practice of raising your voice becomes paramount. The power of advocacy cannot be understated—stand up, speak out, and ensure your concerns are heard. Equip yourself with knowledge of the laws and rights that safeguard your well-being within the workplace.

I have had to assert my voice in establishing ERGs within organizations. While organizations readily formed groups for identities that aligned with the majority, such as the women's ERG and LGBTQIA+/Pride ERG, creating ERGs for underrepresented groups faced significant resistance. Initiatives like the Black ERG, Latino/Hispanic ERG, Diverse-Abled ERG, and Asian ERG encountered strong pushback, requiring me to not only use my voice but also risk my job, status, and reputation to advocate for their creation, often facing repeated denials.

Despite presenting numerous case studies, facts, and figures emphasizing the return on investment (ROI) of DEI and the business case for diversity, these efforts were met with resistance. The process demanded exhaustive efforts, compelling me to utilize every resource available to champion these groups. Some were eventually established during my tenure after persistent advocacy, but others only came into existence long after I had left the organization.

The reality is that we must fight. Fighting means knowing your laws and knowing your rights. Importantly, amidst the fight and the pursuit of equity, remember to find moments of respite.

Understand that self-care and rest are not signs of weakness but vital strategies to ensure your sustainability and resilience in the battle for justice. The reality is that rest is not always enough. It is essential to learn the concept of radical rest. We must imagine, instill, inspire, increase. Another solution is radical rest. Taking time to rethink.

According to Tricia Hersey, author of *The Nap Ministry*, rest is key. Taking time to rest leads to innovation, which leads to more productivity. At the same time, we need to be careful of the word productivity. The term productivity is typically associated with efficiency, output, and the accomplishment of tasks within a specific period. It tends to emphasize continuous effort and measurable results. The idea of productivity is not always conducive to rest because it implies a focus on constant action and output, which can be at odds with the concept of taking a pause, allowing oneself to recharge, and promoting well-being. In a culture that highly values productivity, there may be a tendency to overlook or undervalue the importance of rest as a critical component of overall health and sustained effectiveness.

There are various strategies to prevent fatigue and alleviate burnout. First, align with the right organizations ready to do the actual work. Second, set realistic expectations about what you need. This can be the difference between driving change through DEI or exhausting teams with unrealistic demands. Third, anticipate growing external issues that might cause fatigue. Create psychological safety and find spaces for yourself and others to get support. Next, be transparent and communicate progress in real-time. This allows employees to be in step with progress rather than providing feedback that they do not know what is going on, creating disengagement. And lastly, prioritize rest, wellness, and mental health. The toll on our mental health and well-being is staggering.

The mental fortitude needs to be revised. The work of DEI is demanding. None of us should be alarmed by fatigue. Instead, we should all be prepared. Preparation starts with safety and equal promotion.

FOSTERING SAFETY

Safety forms the bedrock of real equity. It goes beyond physical security, encompassing emotional and psychological well-being. An equitable workplace prioritizes an environment where all individuals, regardless of their background, feel safe expressing their opinions, concerns, and identities. It is about nurturing an inclusive sanctuary where micro-aggressions, discrimination, and biases are challenged and addressed swiftly. When employees feel genuinely safe, they are empowered to contribute to their authentic selves, leading to more prosperous collaboration, innovation, and overall job satisfaction.

Reflecting on my career journey, I realize that there were only a few individuals I felt comfortable approaching with basic questions. However, a pervasive fear held me back, as I worried about potentially upsetting the status quo or being stereotyped. I was afraid of being perceived as a complainer, lazy, ignorant, or unprepared – feelings I already grappled with internally, making vulnerability seem impossible. Consequently, I did not feel safe expressing my true self at work. As I entered new life stages, like marriage and parenthood, I hesitated to bring personal experiences to the workplace. I would not even bring photos for my desk to work. I practiced keeping my poker face and staying in my lane.

This fear of vulnerability and the perceived need to safeguard myself hindered my career growth. I spent more time protecting myself than focusing on productivity and professional development. Consequently, my reluctance to seek help became a significant obstacle to advancing in my career.

Safety and security, in the context of equity, means ensuring fair treatment and protection against discrimination or retaliation. An equitable workplace is one where employees do not fear reprisals for speaking out against injustice. It is about establishing transparent policies that safeguard against discriminatory actions and provide mechanisms for addressing grievances. Security also extends to pay equity, where every individual, irrespective of their background, is compensated fairly for their skills and contributions.

EQUAL PROMOTION AND OPPORTUNITY

Solving the dilemma involves equal promotions and opportunities. Actions speak louder than words. If you are a leader reading this, you must provide the opportunities that will enable true success.

A key aspect of measuring equity lies in evaluating the opportunities available to employees. An equitable workplace offers every individual an equal chance to earn a living wage, grow professionally, and prosper within the organization. This means dismantling barriers that hinder advancement based on factors like gender, ethnicity, or socio-economic background.

Equity within the workplace is about providing equal access to growth and advancement opportunities. These opportunities ensure that promotions and career paths are determined by merit rather than biased assumptions. Being able to care for our families means more than achieving the ultimate goal; it involves leaving a legacy and having the ability to catch up.

The pinnacle of a successful diversity and inclusion effort is reflected in equal promotion and growth opportunities for all employees. In an equitable workplace, promotions are based on skills, qualifications, and potential rather than on favoritism or implicit biases. When diversity is genuinely embraced, it manifests in leadership teams that reflect a rich tapestry of backgrounds and perspectives. An equitable organization ensures that each employee, regardless of their identity, has a genuine shot at climbing the corporate ladder, contributing to a more dynamic and representative leadership.

Measuring real equity involves adopting an integrated approach that transcends statistics and optics. It means going beyond counting heads to understanding hearts and minds. Real equity is not achieved through surface-level tokenism; it thrives when every individual within the organization feels valued, respected, and empowered. It is a journey that necessitates ongoing self-assessment, active listening, and continuous improvement.

In conclusion, it is imperative to erect the pillars of safety, security, and equal opportunity as the foundation for learning and measuring genuine equity. When these pillars are firmly in place, they foster an environment where diversity not only thrives but goes beyond mere percentages and spreadsheets. Instead, it manifests in a vibrant, inclusive culture that not only celebrates differences but actively dismantles barriers. As organizations navigate the complexities of measuring equity, they contribute to a future where every employee, regardless of their background, has an equal opportunity for prosperity, advancement, and fulfillment.

The goal is to change systems and the solution is real equity. We must empower ourselves to obtain positions of power, so we do not have to ask permission to be included. The solution goes back to Coretta Scott King. While she made numerous inspiring statements throughout her life, she emphasized the importance of continuing the struggle for justice and equality across generations. According to Mrs. King, "Struggle is a never-ending process. Freedom is never really won; you earn it and win it in every generation."

Rev. Dr. Martin Luther King, Jr., Malcolm X, and Marcus Garvey knew and understood that they had to use laws and policies to make long-standing changes to laws and hearts. The real dilemma is that diversity must be detached from race, gender, and other social constructs that bind us to be able to sustain ourselves without being accepted. We must imagine a different world for our children and the next generation in our workplaces and communities.

Our similarities outweigh our differences. Ultimately, we must fight for a better world. We all have the power to change the world one equitable decision at a time. Only that way will we find the opposite of a dilemma, a resolution, or a solution. While a dilemma refers to a situation in which one must choose between two or more equally challenging options, a resolution signifies the act of finding an answer or making a decision that resolves the problem at hand.

Ultimately, the goal is for each of us to achieve a deep mastery of DEI. We should reach a point where conflicting choices no longer breed uncertainty or dilemmas but instead become opportunities for profound growth and transformation.

APPENDIX

RESOURCES

7 Reasons You Might Quit Your DEI Leadership Role This Year. Senior Executive. https://seniorexecutive.com/reasons-you-might-quit-your-dei-leadership-role-this-year/

Black consumers empowered by "selfless" spending. Nielsen IQ. https://nielseniq.com/global/en/insights/analysis/2022/black-consumers-empowered-by-selfless-spending/

Combs, Gene. "White Privilege: What's A Family Therapist to Do?" Journal of Marital and Family Therapy, vol. 45, no. 1, 2019,

Culture Amp research reveals striking disconnect between organizations' commitment and action on DEI | Culture

DEI in 2022: Key trends and findings | Culture Amp. https://www.cultureamp.com/workplace-dei-report-2022

Disparities in Debt: Why Debt Is a Driver in the Racial Wealth Gap." 2022 https://core.ac.uk/download/539980512.pdf.

Haile, Nardos, and Karena Phan. "Megan Thee Stallion Shooting Trial Exposes Hazards of Misogynoir. "The Charlotte Post, vol. 49, no. 17, 2022.

Hasbrouck, Brandon. "Movement Constitutionalism." 2022, https://core.ac.uk/download/543562070.pdf

Hays, P. A. (2001). Addressing cultural complexities in practice: A framework for clinicians and counselors. Washington, DC: American Psychological Association.

Hersey, T. (2022). Rest is resistance: THE INSTANT NEW YORK TIMES BESTSELLER. Hachette UK.

Gordon, S. A. (2021). UNBIAS: Addressing Unconscious Bias at Work. John Wiley & Sons.

Hays, P. A. (2001). Addressing cultural complexities in practice: A framework for clinicians and counselors. Washington, DC: American Psychological Association.

Kendi, I. X. (2017). Stamped from the Beginning: The Definitive History of Racist Ideas in America. Random House.

LinkedIn's analysis of C-suite hiring patterns https://www.linkedin.com/pulse/from-diversity-data-10-roles-rising- fastest-c-suite-hiring-anders/

Lowe, Toni Howard. Overcoming DEI Leadership Challenges https://www.linkedin.com/learning/overcoming-dei-leadership-challenges/the-power-you-hold-in-dei?u=111018796

McKinsey – The Emerging Black American Consumer https://www.mckinsey.com/featured-insights/diversity-and-inclusion/a-300-billion-dollar-opportunity-serving-the-emerging-black-american-consumer.

Monster Work Watch Report. https://learnmore.monster.com/monster-work-watch-report

Positioning Your Chief Diversity Officer for Top Performance. Russell Reynolds Associates. https:// www.russellreynolds.com/en/insights/articles/positioning-chief-diversity-officer-top-performance

Race-Based Traumatic Stress | Fact Sheet - ABCT - Association for Behavioral and Cognitive Therapies. https://www.abct.org/fact-sheets/race-based-traumatic-stress/

Steele, J. M. A CBT approach to internalized racism among African Americans. International Journal for the Advancement of Counselling. (2020)

Thatch, Thela. Special Diversity Panel Write-Up in the LA Times: LA Times Panel Discussion the ESG Effect. (2022)

The Black consumer: A $300 billion opportunity. McKinsey. https://www.mckinsey.com/featured-insights/diversity-and-inclusion/a-300-billion-dollar-opportunity-serving-the-emerging-black-american-consumer.

The Korn Ferry Survey of Professionals: https://www. kornferry.com/about-us/press/the-chief-diversity-officer-role-continues-to-gain-importance.

The Sponsorship Dividend: https://coqual.org/reports/ the-sponsor-dividend/

What is Equal Employment Opportunity (EEO)? https://resources.workable.com/hr-terms/what-is-eeo

Whiteness theory - Wikipedia. https://en.wikipedia.org/wiki/Whiteness_theory.

Wisconsin Imprisons 1 in 36 Black Adults, the Highest Rate in the US (pbswisconsin.org) https://pbswisconsin.org/news-item/wisconsin-imprisons-1-in-36-black-adults-the-highest-rate-in-the-us/

Professional Influences From:

April Colbert-Ramirez; Avis Jenkins; Celestine Palmer; Cornell University; David Duran; Doug Freeman; Dr. Anna Nikki Douglas, Dr. Gregory Campbell; Dr. Dana-Marie Thomas; Dr. Deanna Kimbrell; Dr. Karen McBride; Dr. Shelton Goode; Dr. Tana Sessions; Dr. Norvell Thomas; Fred Smith; Genevieve Michel Bryan, Isabel Wilkerson; Joy Atkinson; Joyce Wall; Kimberlee King; Laura Florin; LaVada English; Michelle Frazier; Michelle Silverstone; Minda Harts; Natasha Bowman; National Association of African-Americans in Human Resources (NAAAHR); Neumann University; Niana Tolbert; Nikole Hannah-Jones; Peggy Klaus; Portia James; Professionals In Human Resources Association (PIHRA); Society of Human Resources Management (SHRM); Stacey Gordon; Toni Howard Lowe; Tricia Hersey; University of Southern Florida; University of West Los Angeles; Verná Myers; Veronica Njodinizeh; Walden University; William Rolack; Yamile Haibi; Zandria Robinson

VOCABULARY

(NOTE: This vocabulary list, although hearty, is not a comprehensive list of all terms used in the book. It is intended to assist in understanding some of the words and phrases that are not as commonplace as other words and phrases.)

40 Acres and a Mule - a special order given in 1865 by Union Army General William Sherman which believed that all individuals were to be afforded land and property – this did not include slaves.

CDO/CHRO - Chief Diversity Officer/Chief Human Resources Officer

Collateral consequences - the negative effects of a criminal conviction.

Colorism - prejudice or discrimination against individuals with a dark skin tone, typically among people of the same ethnic or racial group (Oxford Dictionary definition)

Credible messengers - community leaders, and advocates and individuals with relevant life experiences whose role is to help transform attitudes and behaviors.

Critical race theory (CRT) - a set of ideas holding that racial bias is inherent in many parts of western society, especially in its legal and social institutions, on the basis of their having been primarily designed for and implemented by White people. (Oxford Dictionary definition)

D & I - Diversity & Inclusion

DEI - Diversity, Equity, and Inclusion (the moniker used for current diversity work in various industries and institutions)

Grind culture- the individual provision of extra work with the intent of achieving success.

Hostile work environment – an environment where the words and actions of a supervisor, manager or coworker negatively or severely impacts another employee's ability to work in a safe space.

Imposter Syndrome (aka Impostor Syndrome or Phenomenon) - the syndrome where individuals struggle with doubt of intellect, skills, or accomplishments among high-achieving individuals, often times feeling the need to be what they are not because of the feeling of inferiority.

Invisible work - refers to the tasks, responsibilities, or contributions that individuals perform but are not easily recognized, acknowledged, or valued. This type of work often involves activities that are crucial for the functioning of a system or organization but may go unnoticed or underappreciated.

VOCABULARY 193

JEDI - Justice, Equity, Diversity, and Inclusion (another moniker used for current diversity work in various industries and institutions)

Mary Tyler Moore Show - a television show about an iconic modern woman who embodied classic American archetypes—White suburban homemaker and independent single woman. (iMDb)

Meritocracy - government or the holding of power by people selected on the basis of their ability. (Oxford Dictionary definition)

Overseer (i.e., Black/Latina/Minority Female Overseer) - a person with supervisory responsibility over someone or something.

Quiet hiring - the idea of hiring temporary, freelance, and contract workers to fill the job vacancies, post COVID-19 epidemic.

Quiet quitting - doing the minimum amount of work needed in a position and not giving extra effort in that position.

She-cession - the increased, forced unemployment of women, seen after the COVID-19 pandemic.

Social constructionism theory - the theory where individuals create themselves outside of any conventional category, based on what they decide themselves to be.

Social identity theory - the theory where people categorize themselves into different social categories to build their own social identity.

"The Great Reflection" - the period, post-COVID-19, where employees took time to self-reflect on priorities and new focuses.

"The Great Reshuffle"- the post - "Great Resignation/Big Quit" - movement of employees not just changing employment, but also changing careers.

"The Great Resignation/The Big Quit" - the mass resignation of employees during the COVID-19 pandemic, unhappy with work/life balance, in search for greater fits and flexibility.

Tokenism - the practice of recruiting a small number of people from underrepresented groups in order to give the appearance of sexual or racial equality within a workforce.

Uncle Tom - a person regarded as betraying their cultural or social allegiance (Oxford Dictionary definition)

Uplift Suasion – the assimilationist racist idea that Black people should act "respectable" – or imitate middle-class white people I order to show white people that they are human and worthy of receiving equal rights.

Whitewashing – a process that denies race and, at the same time, promotes White culture.

ABOUT THE AUTHOR

Dr. Thelá Thatch, known as Dr. Thelá, is a trailblazing force in the field of equity and transformation, bringing over two decades of expertise in human resources, talent management, organizational development, and diversity and inclusion. As the founder and Chief Equity Officer of Thelá Thatch Consulting, she has finely honed her skills to become a visionary catalyst for positive change.

In her impactful career, Dr. Thelá has held key roles, including executive consultant for the Los Angeles County Department of Health Services, where she crafted pioneering human capital strategies to empower individuals serving the homeless and vulnerable. Her influence extended to notable companies such as Live Nation Entertainment, where she spearheaded the first-ever diversity program in a global organization of over 10,000 employees, and Paychex, where she served as Head of DEI.

Dr. Thelá earned her doctorate in Public Policy and Administration with a specialization in Law from Walden

University. Currently contributing as a faculty member and doctoral dissertation coach at Walden University, she also imparts knowledge as an adjunct professor teaching leadership, organizational development, and DEI at the University of West Los Angeles, Cal State Long Beach, and Neumann University.

A published author with works such as the children's book *The Dog Chef* and the HR book *Employee Handbooks 101*, Dr. Thelá explores the impact of diversity on society, culture, and communities. Her visionary contributions include MRS HR in a Box©, a comprehensive virtual learning and resource system simplifying HR management through cutting-edge technology.

As a co-creator of Inclusionomics™, a podcast and collective think tank, Dr. Thelá is dedicated to driving positive change in the progression of women and other underrepresented professionals. She actively participates in boards and committees, supporting initiatives in Africa, Central America, and her local community. Dr. Thelá has been featured as a writer in esteemed publications like Upscale Magazine, Black Enterprise Magazine, and the LA Times. Additionally, she serves as a keynote speaker, panelist, and moderator.

Dr. Thelá's honors and recognitions reflect her commitment to excellence:

- Top 50 CDOs Powerlist 2023
- Woman of Achievement 2023
- 2022 Women of COLOR DEI Innovator
- 2022 World's Most Ethical Companies Committee Member
- 2022 Paychex Integrity Icon
- Tech Diversity Magazine's Distinguished Diversity Professional 2016
- Top 100 HR Experts to follow on Twitter 2012

For inquiries, kindly reach out to Dr. Thelá through ThelaThatch.com or via email at info@thelathatch.com.

Made in the USA
Coppell, TX
28 February 2024